# Contents

# Planning Ahead

## WHEN TO GO

Fall is generally thought the best time to visit New York. In August many New Yorkers are driven out of town by the searing heat. However, during this time lines are shorter, restaurant reservations optional and outdoor festivals at their peak. The city has occasional blizzards in winter, but these rarely cause disruption.

### TIME

New York is on Eastern Standard Time, three hours ahead of Los Angeles and five hours behind the UK.

## AVERAGE DAILY TEMPERATURES

| JAN | FEB | MAR | APR | MAY | JUN | JUL | AUG | SEP | OCT | NOV | DEC |
|-----|-----|-----|-----|-----|-----|-----|-----|-----|-----|-----|-----|
| 39°F | 41°F | 46°F | 61°F | 70°F | 81°F | 84°F | 82°F | 77°F | 66°F | 54°F | 39°F |
| 4°C | 5°C | 8°C | 16°C | 21°C | 27°C | 29°C | 28°C | 25°C | 19°C | 12°C | 4°C |

**Spring** (March to May) is unpredictable—even in April snow showers can alternate with shirtsleeves weather—but the worst of winter is over by mid-March.
**Summer** (June to August) can be extremely hot and humid, especially July and August.
**Fall** (September to November) sees warm temperatures persisting into October.
**Winter** (December to February) can be severe, with heavy snow, biting winds and sub-freezing temperatures.

## WHAT'S ON

**January/February** *Chinese New Year parades* (✉ Chinatown).
**17 March** *St. Patrick's Day Parade* (✉ Fifth Avenue, 44th–86th streets).
**March/April** *Easter Parade* (✉ Fifth Avenue, 44th–59th streets).
**April–October** *Baseball season* (► 49, 85).
**May** *Ninth Avenue International Food Festival* (✉ Ninth Avenue, 37th–57th streets ☎ 800/894–9166).
*Martin Luther King Day Parade* (3rd Sun ✉ Fifth Avenue, 44th–86th streets).
**June** *Metropolitan Opera park concerts* (☎ 212/870–7492).
*JVC Jazz Festival* (✉ various venues ☎ 212/501–1390).
*Lesbian and Gay Pride Parade* (✉ Fifth Avenue, Midtown to Washington Square).
**4 July** *Independence Day* (► 84).
**July–August** *Shakespeare in the Park* (✉ Delacorte Theater ☎ 212/539–8750).
*NY Philharmonic park concerts* (☎ 212/875–5709).
**August** *Harlem Week* (☎ 212/427–7200).
**August–September** *Lincoln Center Out-of-Doors Festival* (☎ 212/875–5400, ► 84).
*US Open Tennis Championships*

(☎ 718/760–6200).
**September** *Feast of San Gennaro* (✉ Little Italy).
**September–October** *New York Film Festival* (✉ Lincoln Center ☎ 212/875–5050).
*Columbus Day Parade* (✉ Fifth Avenue, 44th–86th streets).
**November** *NYC Marathon* (✉ Staten Island to Central Park ☎ 212/860–2280).
*Macy's Thanksgiving Day Parade* (✉ Central Park West, 81st Street ☎ 212/494–5432).
**December** *Tree Lighting Ceremony* (✉ Rockefeller Center ☎ 212/632–3975).
*New Year's Eve celebrations* (✉ Times Square).

*C. Sherman*

Top 25 locator map
(continues on inside
back cover)

◄

# CityPack
# New York *Top 25*

**KATE SEKULES**

If you have any comments or
suggestions for this guide you
can contact the editor at
*Citypack@the AA.com*

**AA Publishing**
Find out more about AA Publishing and the
wide range of services the AA provides by
visiting our web site at *www.theAA.com*

# About This Book

## ORGANIZATION

This guide is divided into six sections:
- Planning Ahead, Getting There
- Living New York City—New York City Now, New York City Then, Time to Shop, Out and About, Walks, New York City by Night
- New York City's Top 25 Sights
- New York City's Best—best of the rest
- Where To—detailed listings of restaurants, hotels, stores and nightlife
- Travel Facts—practical information

In addition, easy-to-read side panels provide fascinating extra facts and snippets, highlights of places to visit and invaluable practical advice.

The colors of the tabs on the page corners match the colors of the triangles aligned with the chapter names on the contents page opposite.

## MAPS

**The fold-out map** in the wallet at the back of this book is a comprehensive street plan of New York City. The first (or only) map reference given for each attraction refers to this map. **The Top 25 locator maps** found on the inside front and back covers of the book itself are for quick reference. They show the Top 25 Sights, described on pages 26–50, which are clearly plotted by number (**1**–**25**, not page number) across the city. The second map reference given for the Top 25 Sights refers to this map.

## NEW YORK CITY ONLINE

**www.livebroadway.com**
Live Broadway offers up-to-the-minute details on show times and tickets, as well as reviews.

**www.citysearch.com**
Helping New Yorkers "make the most of their city," City Search has links to and listings for attractions, entertainment, restaurants, shopping, hotels and more. Also has news, reviews and a directory offering NYC information.

**www.nyc.gov**
As the official homepage of the City of New York, the site offers links to the Office of the Mayor as well as information about community services, legal policies, city agencies, news and weather.

**www.ny.com**
Billing itself as "the paperless guide to New York City," ny.com's "How, Wow and Now" sections let you know what's up on New York's entertainment, dining and nightlife scene. The sports section lists forthcoming professional sporting events.

**www.nysale.com**
Information on sample sales, showroom sales, warehouse sales and clearance sales.

**www.nytimes.com**
Here you'll get an inside look at one of the world's most respected newspapers. The site has links to sections covering everything from world affairs to sports and local gossip.

**www.nycvisit.com**
The official tourism website. Includes calendar of events, accommodations information, updates on laws, transit, and lots more.

**www.timessquare.nyctourist.com**
All about Times Square and the area around, Broadway and its theaters in particular; with booking information.

### GOOD TRAVEL SITES

**www.fodors.com**
A complete travel-planning site. You can research prices and weather; book air tickets, cars and rooms; pose questions to fellow travelers and find links to other sites.

**www.iloveny.com**
Official NY State site. Information about touring the region, Catskill Mountains to Niagara Falls.

**www.mta.info**
The Metropolitan Transportation Authority updates you on service changes and any disruptions, and answers all your questions relating to the city's buses and subway. Schedules, maps and fares.

### CYBERCAFÉS
**Cyber World Café**
✉ 139 4th Avenue
(at 14th Street)
☎ 212/254–9922
◉ Daily 6am–9pm

**Kinko's** have locations throughout the city, many open 24 hours.
☎ 800–2–KINKOS

**Starbucks** now provide wireless hookups, a service that is proliferating in the city.

# Getting There

Visitors to New York from outside the US must have a full passport and a return ticket. For countries participating in the Visa Waiver Program, a visa is not required, though you must fill out the green visa-waiver form issued on the plane. You are also required to fill out a customs form and an immigration form.

## MONEY

The unit of currency is the dollar (=100 cents). Notes (bills) come in denominations of $1, $5, $10, $20, $50 and $100; coins come in 25¢ (a quarter), 10¢ (a dime), 5¢ (a nickel) and 1¢ (a penny).

$5

$10

$50

$100

## ARRIVING

New York has three airports—John F. Kennedy (⊠ Queens, 15 miles (24km) east of Manhattan ☎ 718/244-4444), Newark (⊠ New Jersey, 16 miles (25km) west ☎ 973/961-6000) and La Guardia (⊠ Queens, 8 miles (13km) east ☎ 718/533-3400). Most international flights arrive at J.F.K.

18 MILES (29KM)

**La Guardia Airport**
8 miles (13km) to city center Bus/minibus 45–60 minutes, $15 ⊠

⊠ **Newark Airport**
16 miles (25km) to city center Bus/minibus 40 minutes, $12–19

⊠ **J.F.K. Airport**
15 miles (24km) to city center Bus/minibus 1 hour, $13–22

### FROM J.F.K.
The journey to Manhattan takes around an hour, depending on traffic. New York Airport Service Express Bus (☎ 718/875-8200) runs every 15–30 minutes, 6am–11pm (cost $13). The SuperShuttle (☎ 212/258-3826) runs to Manhattan on demand 24 hours a day (cost $13–22). To reserve, use the courtesy telephone next to the Ground Transportation Desk. There is also a free shuttle bus to the A train on the MTA subway. A taxi costs $35 plus tolls and tip. Use only a licensed cab from the official taxi stand. An express rail service between J.F.K. and midtown is under construction but is not expected to be open for at least two years.

### FROM NEWARK
The journey to Manhattan takes around 60 minutes, depending on traffic. Olympia Airport Express (☎ 212/964-6233) runs to Grand Central and the Port Authority every 20 minutes 6am–midnight (less frequently midnight–6am; cost $12). SuperShuttle (☎ 212/315-3006) runs a minibus to Midtown Manhattan 7am–11pm (cost $15–19). A taxi costs about $55, plus tolls.

## From La Guardia
The journey to Manhattan takes between 45 and 60 minutes. SuperShuttle (➤ 6) runs a shared minibus 8am–11pm (cost $15). Services to Manhattan are also provided by New York Airport Service Express (cost $10). Taxis cost $16–26, plus tolls and tip.

## Arriving by Bus
Greyhound buses from across the US and Canada and commuter buses from New Jersey arrive at the Port Authority Terminal (✉ 42nd Street at Eighth Avenue ☎ 212/564–8484).

## Arriving by Train
Commuter trains use Grand Central Terminal (✉ 42nd Street at Park Avenue ☎ 212/532–4900). Long-distance trains arrive at Pennsylvania Station (✉ 31st Street at Eighth Avenue ☎ 212/582–6875). PATH trains from New Jersey stop at several stations in the city.

## Getting Around
New York's subway system has 466 stations, many open 24 hours (those with a green globe outside are always staffed). To ride the subway you need a Metrocard, which you can refill. Unlimited ride Metrocards are also available; with these you must wait 18 minutes between swipes. Swipe the card to enter the turnstile. Many stations have separate entrances for up- and downtown services. Make sure you take a local train, not a restricted-stop express.

Bus stops are on or near corners, marked by a sign and a yellow painted curb. Any length of ride costs the same as the subway, and you can use a Metrocard, or correct change ($2). Bus maps are available from token booth clerks in subway stations.

A yellow cab is vacant when the central number on the roof is illuminated and the "Off Duty" side lights are not. All cabs display current rates on the door, have a meter inside and can supply a printed receipt.

For more information on public transportation and driving in New York ➤ 91.

### INSURANCE
Check your insurance coverage and buy a supplementary policy if needed. A minimum of $1 million medical cover is recommended. Choose a policy that also includes trip cancellation, baggage and document loss.

### VISITORS WITH DISABILITIES
City law requires that all facilities constructed after 1987 provide complete access to people with disabilities. Many owners of older buildings have willingly added disability-access features as well. Two important resources for travelers with disabilities are the Mayor's Office for People with Disabilities (✉ 100 Gold Street, second floor ☎ 212/788–2830) and Hospital Audiences' guide to New York's cultural institutions, called Access for All (☎ 212/575–7660). This $5 book describes the accessibility of each place and includes information on hearing and visual aids, alternative entrances and the height of telephones and water fountains. H.A. also provides descriptions of theater performances on audio cassettes for people with visual impairments.

# Living
# New York City

# New York City Now

Above: *Times Square*
Right: *A New York traffic cop on patrol*

After 11 September, 2001, New York was in flux for quite a while. Suddenly Gotham City was no longer impermeable, and its trademark *chutzpah*, brashness, glitz and glamour seemed disrespectful at best. In the weeks following that unspeakable day, the spirit of New Yorkers, and therefore of New York, was clearly on display as all 8 million residents shared the pain of the thousands bereaved or directly affected by the World Trade Center's tragic destruction.

You might call that quality "heart." It is what generates the distinctive buzz of New York—a buzz that did come bounding back. At first New York's heart was apparent in impromptu memorials that sprang up on every corner, and in the way people suddenly looked right into others' faces on the subway, or offered a corner of their cramped apartment to a displaced stranger. In time, it was seen in the way New York simply got back to business. And many months and a new mayor later, Manhattan is almost its old self

Above: *The Guggenheim Museum, as famous for its building as its works of art*
Left: *Kors, a new designer store in SoHo*

### 9/11

● "Since nine-eleven…" That was how every sentence began for weeks following the most despicable terrorist act in modern history. Within a day or two, New Yorkers had coined this shorthand for the horror, grief and utter incomprehension that had attacked them. Of the estimated 3,000 victims, 343 were firefighters, consumed by the 2,000° furnace that still burned two months later. The emergency number was never more poignant: 911.

### BASEBALL

● In a city that's mad for baseball, fans cling loyally to "their" teams. The Yankees play at Yankee Stadium, in the Bronx, and the Mets play at Shea Stadium, in Queens. When the teams face off—as they did for the 2000 World Series—it's said to be a Subway Series, one in which fans can travel back and forth from the stadiums using the underground network of trains.

11

Above: *Taking a break in Katz's Deli*
Right: *A seafood restaurant in Chelsea*

## COLOR CHANGE

• The spire of the Empire State Building is bathed in lights whose colors change to honor significant holidays: green on St. Patrick's Day; red for Valentine's Day; yellow and white during Easter week; red, white and blue on Independence Day; blue and white at Chanukah; and red and green for Christmas.

again—but there are some definite changes. Clearly, the boom is over and the coffers are low. New restaurants, hotels, shops, clubs and bars are still opening, but not at such breakneck speed as they once were, and there is a certain edge of fear or caution according to the news of the day. New York is somewhat subdued.

But don't let that worry you. Even a subdued New York runs at top speed and double volume. Arriving today, it's still easy to see why people routinely fall in love with the place. The energy, the vibe, the spirit is intact. Manhattan is built on a vortex magnetic to those who thrive on adrenaline, and New Yorkers seem to walk faster than anyone else on earth—with miraculously few collisions. They have much in common, but there is no single style of a New Yorker. The city is home to people from across the globe, a microcosm of the world condensed into one locale. It is a city that celebrates its differences

and prides itself on the diversity of the people who shape its culture.

No two parts of the city are alike either: one minute you're visiting the designer shops along Madison and Fifth avenues on the Upper East Side, the next you're in West Chelsea's art district, full of galleries in converted factories,

Center: *A basketball game on Seventh Avenue*
Above: *Tavern on the Green, Central Park*

## WHAT'S THAT NEIGHBORHOOD?

• Almost every ten square blocks of Manhattan has a name. Here are just a few: **Battery Park City:** the development on the southwest tip. **Chelsea:** the west teens to twenties; a gay male mecca and (way west) gallery land. **Diamond Row:** Orthodox Hasidic Jews forge jewels here: 47th Street (Fifth/Sixth avenues). **East Village:** East Side from Houston to 14th, once for those priced out of Greenwich Village, now expensive bohemia. **Flatiron:** the former photo district, now Silicon Alley and the trendy restaurants of Park Avenue South. **Garment District:** the heart of the city's fashion industry: 28th–42nd streets, around Seventh Avenue. **Girl Ghetto:** an area of cheap rents east of Second Avenue, north of 68th Street. **Hell's Kitchen:** Midtown, way west. Named in the late 19th century. **Little Italy:** virtually reduced to one street: Mulberry (Spring Street to Canal Street). **Nolita:** in the area "North of Little Italy," the main drag is Elizabeth Street—all trendy, tiny boutiques. **SoHo:** "South of Houston" was the first made-up name to stick. **TriBeCa:** the "Triangle Below Canal" is all lofts and restaurants.

Above: *Grand Central Oyster Restaurant*
Above right: *The Rockefeller Center concourse*
Right: *Taking the baby for a run in Central Park*
Far right: *SoHo's cast-iron buildings* (top) *and shoe-shiners outside Grand Central Terminal* (below)

## PARADE TIME

• Almost every large ethnic group in New York mounts an annual parade, such as the St. Patrick's Day Parade and June's Puerto Rican Day Parade. The venue is usually Fifth Avenue. Most have political or religious roots, but everyone enjoys the music, food and dance.

then, down a few blocks, you're in the cobbled streets of the Meatpacking district, with its antiques stores and restaurants. Needless to say, the pace of change is fast—it wasn't long ago that SoHo, with its Prada and Chanel stores, was where to find the art galleries, and the Meatpacking district was where meat was packed. In fact, for the time being, it still is; the old and the new coexist here.

The city really does never sleep. Cabs and subways run all night, and there are plenty of late-night bars and 24-hour delis and diners. Wherever you look, something is happening—an acappella group on a street corner, a wildly-colored mural on the side of a building, an intense pick-up basketball game. It is a city to be taken in with all of your senses. It requires an adventurous spirit and a passion for exploring. You are guaranteed to spot at least one thing you've never seen before, as well as

Living **New York City**

much that is thrillingly familiar from all the movies and songs it's inspired.

The past few years have seen a massive clean-up in the infrastructure of what was once a crime-prone city, and, despite the economic downturn, present-day New York remains slick and pleasant and fully-functional. Mayor Bloomberg continued Giuliani's hygienic policies when he banned smoking in all bars and restaurants in March 2002. That and a general tightening up of surveillance and security are in danger, some say, of sanitizing the city a little *too* much. But there's really no cause for concern: More than any city on earth, the only constant in New York is change.

### TIMES SQUARE

● You know you're in Times Square when brightly lit electric billboards, television screens and adverts beckon from every direction. The area used to be riddled with grime and crime, but thanks to clean-up initiatives in the 1990s it is now a hub of culture, nightlife and glamour, with Broadway theaters, elegant hotels and plenty of stores. Each year on 31 December thousands of revelers gather in Times Square to see the New Year ushered in.

fff15

# New York City Then

Left to right: *A 1664 plan of Manhattan, Long Island, the Hudson River and New Amsterdam; British troops enter New York; George Washington; the unveiling of the Statue of Liberty; Prohibition ends, allowing the first legal wine delivery for 14 years*

### THE FIGHT FOR INDEPENDENCE

In 1664 Wall Street's wall failed to deter the British, who invaded Manhattan Island and named it New York. Almost 100 years later, in 1763, the Treaty of Paris gave the British control over 13 American colonies. In 1770 the Sons of Liberty fought the British at the Battle of Golden Hill and in 1776 the American Revolutionary War began and the British chose New York as their headquarters. The Declaration of Independence was read at Bowling Green in July 1776 and the Treaty of Paris ended the war in 1783.

**Pre-1600** New York is populated by Native American groups.

**1609** Henry Hudson sails up the Hudson seeking the North West Passage.

**1625** "Nieuw Amsterdam" is founded by the Dutch West India Company. A year later the colony's leader buys Manhattan Island from the Native Americans for $24 of trinkets.

**1664** The British invade.

**1774** New York "Tea Party"—tax rebels empty an English tea clipper into New York harbor.

**1776** American Revolutionary War begins.

**1783** War ends. Two years later New York becomes capital of the United States.

**1789** George Washington is sworn in as first US president at Federal Hall.

**1790** Philadelphia becomes US capital.

**1807** Robert Fulton launches his first steamboat, creating trade routes that make many New Yorkers' fortunes.

**1827** Slavery in New York is abolished.

**1848** Start of first great immigrant waves.

**1861** New York backs the Union during the Civil War.

**1868** The first "El" (elevated train) opens.

**1886** The Statue of Liberty is unveiled.

**1892** Ellis Island opens.

**1904** New York's first subway opens.

**1929** The Great Depression begins.

**1933** Prohibition ends. Fiorello La Guardia becomes mayor.

**1954** Ellis Island is closed down.

**1964** Race riots in Harlem and Brooklyn.

**1975** A federal loan saves New York City from bankruptcy.

**1987** Stock market crashes.

**1990** David Dinkins, New York's first black mayor, takes office.

**2001** Terrorists fly two hijacked passenger planes into the World Trade Center twin towers, destroying them and killing an estimated 3,000 people.

**2002** Rudy Giuliani's term as mayor ends. Michael Bloomberg takes office.

**TENEMENT LIFE**

As you make your first explorations in New York, consider how it was for the early immigrants, especially those who were herded through Ellis Island, then crammed into Lower East Side tenements. Imagine how daunting the cast iron-framed SoHo buildings must have appeared to someone from, say, Vienna. Although they are now the scene of costly loft living, or home to chain stores or swank boutiques, during the immigrant boom they were sweatshop skyscrapers—symbols of hope for a fresh future.

17

# Time to Shop

## WINDOW-SHOPPING

Even if you can't afford to buy anything from Manhattan's most upscale stores, no visit to New York is complete without window-shopping. Start on Lexington Avenue between 59th and 60th streets: you'll see flags waving outside the legendary Bloomingdale's department store. Walk west to Madison Avenue: between 60th and 61st streets is Barney's, for expensive cutting-edge clothing, jewelry, accessories and a basement of beauty products. (Don't miss the wacky Christmas windows.) Walk west along 57th Street, past Chanel and Christian Dior, to the prestigious department stores Henri Bendel and Bergdorf Goodman. On Fifth Avenue peer in at Gucci, Tiffany's and Prada.

Thought there was nothing you couldn't buy over the internet? Think again! New York is a shopping haven, with clothing, furniture, food and souvenirs available no place else.

Shopping is still one of the best ways to get an inside look at life in New York—its trends, fads, pace, cultural influences and sense of humor. From massive department stores to small, family-owned downtown boutiques, the city has something for everyone.

You can find all kinds of NYC paraphernalia—from Statue of Liberty coin banks and taxicab neckties to sweatshirts bearing the New York Police Department initials and Yankee baseball caps—throughout the city. Gift shops at the major museums offer reproductions, posters, jewelry, stationery and commemorative items.

For fashion head for Nolita and SoHo, where small (and often expensive) boutiques line the streets. Major franchises (Old Navy, Banana Republic, Pottery Barn) can also be found here, along Broadway, and side streets such as Prince Street, Broome Street and Spring Street.

If you're planning a night out on the town, try the stores along 8th Street, starting on Broadway and heading west. These are popular among young clubbers—mannequins in the storefronts flaunt outrageously sexy garb.

Music lovers will find no shortage of places to browse, whether looking for current chart-toppers or something from the past. CDs, DVDs and videos are available at major chain stores such as Tower Records and Virgin, where sales are common. In the Village, smaller music stores carry vintage records, tapes and CDs at prices ranging from a few dollars to several hundred for collectors' editions.

If you are looking for a bargain, look no further than the city's popular sample sales, where designer brands are marked down as much as 80 percent. Designer sales are often held at open showrooms over a few days. Arrive early on the first day of the sale for the best selection, though prices do drop as days go by. To learn about sample sales pick up *New York Magazine* or *Time Out New York,* or log onto www.daily-candy.com or www.mysale.com. For electronic goods try J&R or PC Richard & Sons, in Circuit City (✉ 232 E86th Street; 52 E14th Street), where sales are often held.

As for food, in addition to the many upscale restaurants and cafés, simple NYC classics like hot dogs, pizza, bagels and frozen yogurt can be found on nearly every street corner, along with food carts purveying anything from hot soft pretzels or candied almonds to six kinds of curry or falafel sandwiches—great street food that can't be beat after a long day of shopping.

*Shoppers in New York can choose from big department stores like Bloomingdale's (above, center) or smaller boutiques*

## FLEA MARKETS

Bric-a-brac is at a premium in New York, where everything has the potential to show up on a movie set. What was for decades the city's main flea market (✉ Around 25th and 26th streets) running every weekend, has gradually been truncated by the construction of residential blocks, and looks set to disappear altogether. For the time being, the indoor market down the street (✉ 112 W25th Street) remains open on the weekends Uptown, check out GreenFlea markets on Saturdays (✉ W84th Street, between Columbus and Amsterdam avenues).

# Out and About

Right: *A Gray Line bus tours Times Square*

Center: *Snug Harbor*

## ORGANIZED SIGHTSEEING
### BOAT TRIPS, BUS TOURS AND GUIDED WALKS

The classic way to orient yourself is to hop on a Circle Line Cruise (☎ 212/563–3200), which circumnavigates Manhattan for three hours, accompanied by a commentary. Pricier, shorter, but more dramatic is a helicopter tour from Helicopter Flight Services (☎ 212/355–0801). In between these extremes are the bus rides organized by Gray Line (☎ 212/397–2620), including Trolley Tours on replicas of 1930s trolleys, and many standard bus-ride-with-commentary orientation trips. Those who enjoy history should join one of Joyce Gold's tours (☎ 212/242–5762).

Many of Seth Kamil and Ed O'Donnell's Big Onion Walking Tours (☎ 212/439–1090) are gastronomic odysseys. This entertaining duo also offer things like the "Riot and Mayhem" tour of civil unrest sites. Another personalized, neighborhood-crunching setup is Adventure on a Shoestring (☎ 212/265–2663), which have been leading walking tours for 40 years. For an insight into one of New York's most fascinating neighborhoods, take a walk—or a jazz, gospel or art tour—with Harlem Heritage (☎ 212/280–7888) and witness the renaissance first hand.

If you want insight into the arts, a few backstage tours are available. The Metropolitan Opera (☎ 212/769–7020) has tours by reservation and Radio City Music Hall (☎ 212/632–4041) offers a Grand Tour Behind the Scenes.

# EXCURSIONS
## STATEN ISLAND
Many Staten Islanders would like to secede from the city—why should they share New York's problems and taxes, they argue, when they not only have their own discrete, rather rural community, but are also completely ignored by all four other boroughs? Whatever the political status, however, the island is a pleasure to visit, especially in summer when all kinds of events are held. Once you've enjoyed the famous ferry ride, buses are the best way to get around.

Snug Harbor is a work in progress—a visual and performance arts center in an 80-acre (32ha) park of 28 historic buildings. Long established here are the Children's Museum and Botanical Garden, as well as a couple of performance venues and a restored row of Greek Revival houses. Both this and historic Richmondtown have a program of summer fairs, concerts and other events. In the exact center of the island, Richmondtown traces 200 years of New York history through restored buildings, craft workshops and costumed re-enactments. There's no better place to get a picture of how New York evolved.

A good use for your Metrocard is to take a ride on the Staten Island train, which takes about 40 minutes to travel its none-too-picturesque route from the ferry to Tottenville and includes a great view of the mighty Brooklyn-bound Verrazano-Narrows Bridge.

Above: *Circle Line offers cruises around Manhattan, as well as a ferry to the Statue of Liberty and Ellis Island*

## INFORMATION

➕ Off map
🚢 Staten Island Ferry (➤ 55)

**Snug Harbor Cultural Center**
✉ 1000 Richmond Terrace
☎ 718/448–2500
🕐 8am–dusk
🚌 S40
🍴 Melville's Café
♿ Good
💵 Free

**Richmondtown**
✉ 441 Clarke Avenue
☎ 718/351–1611
🕐 Wed–Sat 10–5, Sun 11–2, Jul–Aug; Wed–Sun 1–5, rest of year
🚌 S74
🍴 Tavern
♿ Good
💵 Inexpensive

# Walks

## INFORMATION

**Distance** 3 miles (5km)
**Time** 3 hours
**Start point** Corner of
Church and Barclay
streets
🚇 E16
🚉 2, 3, Park Place; A, C
Chambers Street
**End point** Greenwich
Village
🚇 D11
🚉 1, 9 Christopher
Street/Sheridan Square

## DOWNTOWN

Standing on Church Street, look south toward what was once the World Trade Center. Walk east on Barclay Street and look to your left for the Gothic Woolworth Building. At City Hall Park turn left onto Broadway, where City Hall, followed by the Tweed Courthouse, come into view on your right.

Walk east through the park and catch a vista of Brooklyn Bridge. Continue north up Centre Street. You come to Cass Gilbert's gilt-pyramid-crowned US Courthouse on Foley Square at the southeast corner of Federal Plaza on your left, the neoclassical New York County Courthouse past Pearl Street on the right, then, past Hogan Street, the Criminal Courts (The Tombs).

Another block, and here's gaudy Canal Street, which you follow east to Mulberry Street. Continue north up this artery of Little Italy and veer west on Prince Street. After two blocks, you're in the Cast Iron Historic District of SoHo. Look at the Little Singer Building opposite as you cross Broadway. Take any route you please west through the cobbled streets of SoHo, heading north on any of these from Mercer to MacDougal to cross Houston Street. Three blocks later, you reach Washington Square, the center of New York University.

Greenwich
Village

Washington
Square

Little Singer
Building

SoHo

Little Italy

Criminal
Courts

US Courthouse

Tweed
Courthouse

City Hall

Woolworth
Building

Brooklyn
Bridge

Fifth Avenue starts at the north side. Look at gated Washington Square Mews (first right), turn left on W8th Street (see MacDougal Alley, first left), and right on Avenue of the Americas (Sixth Avenue). Keep heading west to reach Greenwich Village (➤ 33).

## MIDTOWN'S GREATEST HITS

Madison Square Garden, behind Penn Station as you exit the subway, is not a garden at all, but a concrete cylinder for sports and concerts. Head two blocks uptown, then take 34th Street east one block to Herald Square, Macy's and Manhattan Mall. Toward the end of the next block, look up to your right. You're underneath the Empire State Building.

Head north up Fifth Avenue. Six blocks brings you to the beaux-arts magnificence of the New York Public Library, with Bryant Park behind. Go east on 42nd Street until you reach Grand Central Terminal, and on the southwest corner of Park Avenue is the Whitney's outpost in the Philip Morris Building. After a look in the Terminal (the Oyster Bar or the Food Court's restaurants can provide refreshment) continue east a block and a half and on the left you'll see the Chrysler Building. Circumnavigate the Terminal, hitting Park Avenue again at 46th Street, with the MetLife building at your back.

A few blocks north you'll find the precursors of the Manhattan skyline: Lever House (northwest of 53rd Street) and Ludwig Mies van der Rohe's Seagram Building (east side, 52nd–53rd streets). Go west on 53rd Street, then south on Madison Avenue to 50th Street, and veer west. Here is Sak's Fifth Avenue (► 73) and St. Patrick's Cathedral, on the right. Straight ahead you'll find the vast Rockefeller Center. If you have the energy and the time head north to Central Park for some more bucolic strolling.

### INFORMATION

**Distance** 3 miles (5km)
**Time** 2 hours
**Start point** Madison Square Garden
🚏 D6
🚇 1, 9 34th Street/Penn Station
**End point** Rockefeller Center
🚏 E2
🚇 B, D, F 47th–50th streets/Rockefeller Center

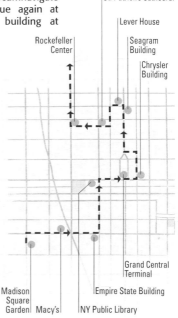

St. Patrick's Cathedral

Lever House

Rockefeller Center

Seagram Building

Chrysler Building

Grand Central Terminal

Madison Square Garden | Macy's

Empire State Building

NY Public Library

# New York City by Night

Above: *The view of Midtown Manhattan, from the lake in Central Park at dusk*
Above right: *Tavern on the Green, Central Park*

## SEE THE LIGHTS

As the sun sets over New York, the city is transformed into an at-once sultry, romantic and mysterious place. Wander through Times Square as the glitzy electric billboards pop out from the dark sky. A stroll, run or bike ride along the banks of the Hudson River on the West Side offers a spectacular view of the sunset and the Statue of Liberty.

## NIGHTLIFE

Clubs and restaurants come to life after dark. As young New Yorkers explore new frontiers in the city, the Meatpacking district—once known for drugs and prostitution—has become gentrified, home to trendy bars and clubs. Celebrity sightings are common at Lotus (✉ 409 W14th Street, at Ninth/Tenth avenues) and Pastis (✉ 9–11 Little W12th Street, at Ninth Avenue). At the other end of the spectrum are biker bars like Hogs-n-Heffers (✉ 859 Washington Street, at W13th Street) and The Village Idiot (✉ 355 W14th Street, at Eighth/Ninth avenues), friendly dives where the beer flows cheaply and the music blares loudly.

## TAKE TO THE WATER

Circle Line Cruises' evening boat rides around Manhattan are a relaxing way to see the world's most famous skyline. Board at Pier 83, at 42nd Street on the Hudson River, or Pier 16, at South Street Seaport. Tour guides on board explain the legends of the city (☎ 212/563–3200).

### FOR A LAUGH

Comedy clubs are a great way to sample New York's sense of humor. Venues such as Caroline's (✉ 1626 Broadway, at 49th Street ☎ 212/757–4100), Comedy Cellar (✉ 117 MacDougal Street, at W3rd/Bleecker streets ☎ 212/254–3480) and Comic Strip Live (✉ 1568 Second Avenue, at 81st/82nd streets ☎ 212/861–9386) are popular. Gotham (✉ 34 W22nd Street, at Fifth Avenue ☎ 212/367–9000) has even been known to host surprise visits from Jerry Seinfeld.

# NEW YORK CITY's
## top 25 sights

The sights are shown on the maps on the inside front cover and inside back cover, numbered **1**–**25** across the city

# Coney Island

## HIGHLIGHTS

- Aquarium
- Boardwalk
- Cyclone
- Nathan's Famous hot dogs
- Sideshow
- Flea market

## INFORMATION

- ✚ Off map; Locator map off C4
- ✉ Surf Avenue, Boardwalk, Brooklyn; Aquarium: W8th Street, Surf Avenue
- ☎ Aquarium 718/265–3474; Sideshow 718/372–5159
- 🕓 Aquarium daily 10–5, summer weekends and holidays 10–7
- 🍴 Cafeteria at Aquarium
- Ⓜ W Stillwell Avenue/ Coney Island
- 🚌 B36, B68
- ♿ Good
- 💲 Aquarium moderate

**Half slummy neighborhood with the skeleton of a fairground, half sunny seashore playground with a wonderful boardwalk, Coney Island is redolent with other people's memories.**

**Nathan's and the Cyclone** At the end of the 19th century, Coney Island on a peak day played host to a million people, attracted by Brooklyn's fresh sea air and by Luna Park, Dreamland and Steeplechase Park fairgrounds. By 1921, a boardwalk and the subway had joined the list of attractions, then 1939–40 added the biggest draw of all, the "Parachute jump." Now in the 21st century, that machine is still there, a rusted ghost like a giant spider on stilts, and the glory days of Luna Park are long since gone, yet seedy Coney Island still draws a crowd. The big-dipper ride, the Cyclone, is still there, more terrifying for rattling of the cars on the wooden track than for the thrill of the ride (although it's not at all bad), and Nathan's Famous hot dogs are still sold from the original site, plus cotton candy, saltwater taffy and corn dogs (deep-fried frankfurters in cornmeal batter).

**Fish and flea market** The New York Aquarium, watery branch of the Bronx Zoo, moved here in 1957. Roughly 10,000 creatures call it home, including beluga whales, coral, a penguin colony and five varieties of shark. It's quite as wonderful as it sounds. The boardwalk Sideshow, though boasting an elastic lady and the blockhead (he hammers nails into his brain), is not such a freak show as it sounds. It's a theatrical performance by East Village arty types.

*The boardwalk along Brighton Beach, Coney Island*

# Statue of Liberty

**The green lady, symbol of the American dream of freedom, takes your breath away, however many times you've seen her photograph—and despite her surprisingly modest stature.**

**How she grew** In the late 1860s, sculptor Frédéric-Auguste Bartholdi dreamed of placing a monument to freedom in a prominent location. His dream merged with the French historian Edouard-René de Laboulaye's idea of presenting the American people with a statue that celebrated freedom and the two nations' friendship. Part of the idea was to shame the repressive French government, but, apparently, New Yorkers took their freedom for granted, and it was only after Joseph Pulitzer promised to print the name of every donor in his newspaper, the *New York World*, that the city's ordinary citizens coughed up the funds to build the statue's pedestal. She was finally unveiled by President Grover Cleveland on 28 October, 1886, in a ceremony from which women were banned.

**Mother of exiles** Emma Lazarus' stirring poem, *The New Colossus*, is engraved on the pedestal, while the tablet reads: July IV MDCCLXXVI— the date of the Declaration of Independence. Beneath her size 107 feet, she tramples the broken shackles of tyranny, and her seven-pointed crown beams liberty to the seven continents and the seven seas.

**What is she made of?** Gustave Eiffel practiced for his later work by designing the 1,700-bar iron and steel structure that supports her. She weighs 225 tons, is 151ft (46m) tall, has an 8-ft (2-m) index finger and a skin of 300 copper plates. The torch tip towers 305ft (93m) above sea level.

## HIGHLIGHTS

- View from the pedestal
- Statue of Liberty Museum
- Fort Wood, the star-shaped pedestal base
- Her new centenary flame

## INFORMATION

- ✚ Off map at E19; Locator map off B4
- ✉ Liberty Island
- ☎ 800/266–1488 or 212/363–3180; www.nps.gov/stli
- 🕐 Daily 9.30–3.30. New security measures mean only the island may be visited
- 🍴 Cafeteria
- Ⓢ 4 Bowling Green, then take the ferry
- 🚌 M1, M6, M15 South Ferry, then take the ferry
- ⛴ Ferry departs Battery Park South Ferry (✚ F19). Ferry information ☎ 212/269–5755
- ♿ Poor
- 💵 Inexpensive
- ↔ Battery Park City (► 13), Ellis Island (► 28), Staten Island Ferry (► 55)
- ❓ Audio tours available

## Ellis Island

### INFORMATION

- ✚ Off map at E19; Locator map off B4
- ✉ Ellis Island
- ☎ 212/363-3200
- 🕐 Daily 9–5, although new security measures mean you should allow extra time for your visit
- 🍴 Café
- 🚇 4 Bowling Green, then take the ferry
- 🚌 M1, M6, M15, then take the ferry
- 🛳 Ferry departs Battery Park South Ferry (✚ F19). Ferry information ☎ 212/269-5755
- ♿ Good
- 💷 Inexpensive
- ↔ Battery Park City (► 13), Statue of Liberty (► 27), Staten Island Ferry (► 55)
- ❓ Audio tours available

**This museum offers a humbling taste of how the huddled masses of new immigrants were not allowed to go free until they'd been herded through these halls, weighed, measured and rubber stamped.**

Half of all America   It was the poor who docked at Ellis Island after sometimes grueling voyages in steerage, since first-class passage included permission to decant straight into Manhattan. Annie Moore, aged 15 and the first immigrant to disembark here, arrived in 1892, followed by 16 million founding fathers over the next 40 years, including such then-fledgling Americans as Irving Berlin and Frank Capra. Half the population of the United States can trace their roots to an Ellis Island immigrant.

Island of tears   The exhibition in the main building conveys the indignities, frustrations and, above all, fears of the arrivals. (As soon as you arrive, collect your free ticket for the half-hour film, *Island of Hope/Island of Tears,* which you'll otherwise end up missing.) You are guided around more or less the same route the millions took: from the Baggage Room, where they had to abandon all they owned; on to the enormous Registry Room, now bare not only of people, but of furniture too; and on through the inspection chambers where medical, mental and political status were ascertained. The Oral History Studio brings it all to life as immigrants recount their experience—especially moving when coupled with the poignant possessions in the "Treasures from Home" exhibit. All this makes for a demanding few hours' sightseeing, which you'll probably be combining with the Statue of Liberty, since the ferries stop at both islands. Wear sensible shoes and bring lunch.

# South Street Seaport

**This reconstructed historic maritime district, with its cobbled streets, is a tourist trap. However, when you stroll the boardwalk on a summer's night, with the moon over the East River, you are very glad to be a tourist.**

**Pier, cruise, shop, eat** The seaside/cruise-ship atmosphere is what's fun at the Pier 17

*The Seaport in the evening*

Pavilion, which juts 400ft (122m) into the East River, overlooking Brooklyn Heights. It's a mall, with chain stores, bad restaurants and a food court, but also three stories of charming wooden decks. The adjoining piers, 16 and 15, harbor a number of historic vessels with picturesque arrangements of rigging, as

well as the replica side-wheeler, *Andrew Fletcher*, and the 1885 schooner, *Pioneer*, which give harbor cruises. Your cash is courted by many stores, housed in the 1812 Federal-style warehouses of Schermerhorn Row—Manhattan's oldest block —and around Water, Front and Fulton streets, and by the cafés in the old Fulton Market.

**Many museums** The Seaport Museum Visitors' Center acts as clearing house for all the small-scale exhibitions here. One ticket admits you to: the second-biggest sailing ship ever built, the *Peking*; the floating lighthouse, *Ambrose*; the Children's Center; the Seaport Museum Gallery; a re-creation of a 19th-century printer's shop; various walking tours and more.

## HIGHLIGHTS

- View of Brooklyn Heights
- Richard Haas' Brooklyn Bridge mural
- Late night forays in the Fulton Fish Market (midnight–8am)
- Boarding *Andrew Fletcher*
- Watching the Wall Street young decant into the bars around 5pm
- *Titanic* Memorial
- Chandlery
- Fulton Market (especially the bakeries)
- Incongruous giant bubble (tennis courts!)
- The sea breeze

## INFORMATION

- ✚ G17; Locator map C4
- ✉ Visitor center: 12 Fulton Street. Tickets also from Pier 16
- ☎ 212/748–8600; www.southseaport.org
- ◉ Fri–Wed 10–6, Jun–Sep; Fri–Wed 10–5, rest of year. Closed 25 Dec and 1 Jan
- 🍴 Numerous
- 🚇 1, 2, 4, 5, J, M, Z Fulton Street; A, C Broadway/ Nassau Street
- 🚌 M15 Pearl/Fulton Street
- ♿ Poor
- 💲 Inexpensive
- ↔ Brooklyn Bridge (➤ 31)
- ❓ Walking tours: "Ship Restoration" and "Back Streets"

**5**

# Best of Brooklyn

**Brooklyn has it all—one of the largest art museums in the US and some of New York's best restaurants; beaches and a park; a zoo and aquarium; hip neighborhoods and avant-garde arts. No wonder everyone's moving here.**

**Big, Bigger, Biggest** If Brooklyn were still a separate city—which it was until 1898—it would be the fourth largest in the US. Home to more than 2 million people, it is the most populous of New York's five boroughs and the most diverse, with Russian, Hasidic, Middle Eastern, Italian and Chinese neighborhoods… you name it. The Brooklyn Museum of Art, intended by McKim, Mead & White to be the biggest museum in the world (it's actually the seventh largest in the US), has collections ranging from pre-Columbian art to 58 Rodin sculptures, plus what many feel are the best Egyptian rooms outside the British Museum (and Egypt). It abuts Prospect Park, opened in 1867 and considered by its designers, Olmstead and Vaux, better than their earlier work, Central Park. The Botanic Garden (pictured above), the zoo and the Bandshell summertime events are highlights.

**BAM!** In Fort Greene stands the Brooklyn Academy of Music, aka BAM. Arguably New York's most exciting cultural institution, BAM boasts cinemas, two theaters, a café with live jazz and eclectic programing. There are many restaurants to discover nearby, as well as in Boerum Hill's Smith Street and Northern Park Slope along Fifth Avenue. Worth exploring are the more established brownstone neighborhoods of Park Slope, Cobble Hill and Brooklyn Heights, the latter famous for the Promenade and its (now poignant) view of downtown Manhattan. It also houses the fantastic Transit Museum.

# Brooklyn Bridge

**With its twin Gothic towers and ballet of cables, the first Manhattan–Brooklyn link fulfils beautifully its symbolic role of affording entry into new worlds of opportunity—and the view from here is spectacular.**

**Killer bridge** In 1869, before construction had even started, the original engineer, John Roebling, had his foot crushed by a ferry and died of gangrene three weeks later. His son, Washington, took over the project, only to succumb to the bends and subsequent paralysis. Washington's wife, Emily Warren, finished overseeing the construction, during which 20 workmen died in various nasty accidents. Then, on 30 May, 1883, a few days after the opening, a woman fell over, screamed, and set off a 20,000-person stampede, which claimed 12 more lives. Robert Odlum's was the first non-accidental bridge-related death. He jumped off for a bet in 1885 and died from internal bleeding later.

**Bridge of sighs** Now, the occasional leaper chooses the cable walk as his or her last, but things are mostly peaceful. The best time and direction to walk the renovated (in 1983) footpath is east from Brooklyn to Manhattan at dusk. The sun sets behind Liberty Island and, as you stroll on, downtown looms larger and larger, the sky darkens to cobalt, the lights go on, the skyline goes sparkly, and you are swallowed into the metropolis. It's a transcendental half-hour. Although you'll almost certainly be fine, it's still not a good idea to walk the bridge late at night, especially carrying cameras. And keep to the downtown side; the other lane is for bikes.

## HIGHLIGHTS

- Walk to Manhattan
- Panorama of NY buildings
- Cables—each of 5,282 wires
- Jehovah's Witnesses' *Watchtower* HQ
- Cars hurtling only yards below your feet
- Cyclists hurtling 6 inches (15cm) from your face

## INFORMATION

- J16; Locator map C4
- Walkway entrance is across Park Row from City Hall Park
- 4, 5, 6 Brooklyn Bridge/ City Hall; J, M, Z Chambers Street
- M1, M6
- Good
- Free
- South Street Seaport (➤ 29)

*Jogging across Brooklyn Bridge*

31

## Chinatown

**New York's Chinatown, the largest in the West, encroaches on Little Italy and the Jewish Lower East Side, even on Hispanic "Loisaida." Wander here and you're humbled by the sight of a lifestyle that, making no concessions to the visitor, continues to thrive.**

Going west  Prefiguring the movement of immigrants from the devolved Russia and Eastern Europe of today, Chinese people first came to New York in the late 19th century, looking to work a while, make some money and return home. But, by 1880 or so, some 10,000 men—mostly Cantonese railroad workers decamped from California—had been stranded between Canal, Worth and Baxter streets. Tongs (sort of secret mafia operations) were formed, and still keep order today over some 150,000 Chinese, Taiwanese, Vietnamese, Burmese and Singaporeans. New York, incidentally, has two more Chinatowns: in Flushing, Queens and Eighth Avenue, Brooklyn, with a further 150,000 inhabitants.

A closed world  Although you may happily wander its colorful, slightly manic streets, you will never penetrate Chinatown. Many of its denizens never learn English, never leave its environs and never wish to. The 600 factories and 350 restaurants keep them in work; then there are the tea shops, mah-jong parlors, herbalists, fishmongers and the highest bank-to-citizen ratio in New York, in which Chinese stash their wages (normally not more than $10–$20,000 a year) to save for the "eight bigs" (car, television, video recorder, fridge, camera, phone, washing machine and furniture), to send home, or eventually to invest in a business of their own.

### HIGHLIGHTS

- Buddhist temple (✉ 64B Mott Street)
- Chinatown History Museum (✉ 70 Mulberry Street)
- Pearl River Mart (✉ 277 Canal Street)
- Doyers Street: once the "Bloody Angle"
- Chinatown Ice Cream Factory (✉ 65 Bayard Street)
- Columbus Park (✉ Bayard/Baxter streets)
- The Tombs, or Criminal Courts Building (✉ 100 Centre Street)
- Cecilia Tam's egg cakes (✉ Mosco/Mott streets)

### INFORMATION

✚ G14; Locator map B4
✉ Roughly delineated by Worth Street/East Broadway, the Bowery, Grand Street, Centre Street
🍴 Numerous (some close around 10pm)
🚇 J, M, Z, N, R, 6, A, C, E, 1, 9 Canal Street; B, D Grand Street
🚌 M1, B51
♿ Poor
↔ Little Italy (➤ 56)
❓ General tours ☎ 212/619–4785; Chinese herbal medicine tours ☎ 212/219–2527

# Greenwich Village

**This sugar-sweet, picturesque, human-scale neighborhood of brownstones and actual trees is one of the romantic images of Manhattan, familiar from sitcoms and movies. Its dense streets are rewarding to wander, and you can take a break in a café or jazz club.**

**What village?** It was named after Greenwich, southeast London, by the British colonists who settled here at the end of the 17th century. In the 18th and early 19th centuries the wealthy founders of New York society took refuge here from smallpox, cholera and yellow fever.

**Bohemia, academe, jazz** When the elite moved on, the bohemian invasion began, pioneered by Edgar Allan Poe, who moved to 85 W3rd Street in 1845. Fellow literary habitués included: Mark Twain, O. Henry, Walt Whitman, F. Scott Fitzgerald, Eugene O'Neill and John Dos Passos. New York University arrived in Washington Square in 1831 and grew into the country's largest private university. Post World War II, bohemia became beatnik; a group of abstract artists, centered around Jackson Pollock, Mark Rothko and Willem de Kooning, also found a home here.

**Freedom parades** Café Society, where Billie Holiday made her 1938 debut, was one of the first non-racially segregated clubs in New York. Thirty years later, a different kind of discrimination was challenged, when police raided the Stonewall Inn on 28 June, 1969, arresting gay men for illegally buying drinks and setting off the Stonewall Riots—the birth of the Gay Rights movement. The Inn was on Christopher Street, which became the main drag (no pun intended) of New York's gay community, and ranked with San Francisco for excitement.

## HIGHLIGHTS

- Cafés
- Jazz clubs
- Washington Square Park
- NYC's narrowest house (✉ 75 Bedford Street)
- West (of Hudson Street) Village
- Halloween Parade
- Jefferson Market Library
- Balducci's (the grocers)
- Minetta Lane
- Carmine Street pool

*Washington Memorial Arch*

## INFORMATION

- ✠ D10; Locator map B3
- ✉ East–west from Broadway to Hudson Street; north–south from 14th Street to Houston Street
- 🍴 Numerous
- Ⓐ A, C, E, B, D, F W4th Street; 1, 9 Christopher Street
- 🚌 M10
- 🅿 PATH Christopher Street
- ♿ Poor

33

# Union Square

## INFORMATION

- ✚ F9; Locator map B3
- ✉ W14th–17th streets, Park Avenue South, Broadway
- ☎ Greenmarket 212/788–7900
- 🕐 Greenmarket Mon, Wed, Fri, Sat 8–6
- 🍴 Numerous
- 🚇 4, 5, 6, L, N, R 14th Street, Union Square
- 🚌 M3
- ♿ Poor

**For proof that New York is always evolving, see Union Square. A "needle park" in the 1970s, it's now where downtown and up meet, with great restaurants, a wild café scene and the egalitarian Greenmarket.**

**Not those Unions** Laid out in 1839, Union Square had close encounters with socialism though its name actually refers to the union of Broadway and Fourth Avenue. It was a mecca for soapbox orators in the first three decades of the 20th century, then, during the 1930 Depression, 35,000 unemployed rallied here en route to City Hall to demand work; workers' May Day celebrations convened here too. Later, Andy Warhol picked up the vibes, set up his factory (on the southwest corner), and began publishing his style mag, *Interview*, where once the *Daily Worker* had been produced.

**Green** In summer, the park teems with office refugees, sharing the lawn with an equestrian George Washington by John Quincy Adams Ward, an Abe Lincoln by Henry Kirke Brown and a Marquis de Lafayette, which Frédéric-Auguste Bartholdi (of subsequent Statue of Liberty fame) gave the city in 1876. Mondays, Wednesdays, Fridays and Saturdays are Greenmarket days. An entire culture, an actual Manhattan lifestyle, has grown around this collation of stalls overflowing with homegrown and homemade produce from New England farmers, fishers, bakers and growers. Everyone has their favorite farmer. Cult highlights include: the maple candies, the Amish cheeses, the Pretzel Man (and his pretzels), the fresh clams, the sugarfree muffins and the hundred blends of mesclun salad. The square also has a huge Barnes and Noble (north) and Virgin Megastore (south).

Top: *The Saturday market in Union Square*

# Empire State Building

**It was not Fay Wray's fault, nor Cary Grant's in *An Affair to Remember*, that this is the most famous skyscraper in the world. Rather, its fame is the reason it has appeared in every New York movie. You have to climb this.**

**King for 40 years** This is the very definition of "skyscraper," and it was the highest man-made thing until the late, lamented World Trade Center went up in the 1970s. Now it is once again the tallest building in New York. Construction began in 1929, not long before the great Wall Street Crash, and by the time it was topped in 1931—construction went at the superfast rate of four stories a week—so few could afford to rent space, they called it "the Empty State Building." Only the popularity of its observatories kept the wolves from the door. These viewpoints still attract 35,000 visitors a day. Many stop off on the Mezzanine for the New York Skyride, which simulates a rooftop flight, minus a hair-raising virtual crash over Wall Street, edited out after 11 September; the tour guide is *Star Trek*'s "Scottie"—James Doohan.

**Facts** It is 1,250ft (381m) high, with 102 floors. The frame contains 60,000 tons of steel, 10 million bricks line the building, and there are 6,500 windows. The speediest of the 73 elevators climb 1,200ft (355m) per minute. The speediest runners in the annual Empire State Run-Up climb almost 170 steps per minute, making the 1,860 steps to the 102nd floor in 11 minutes—though normal people take about half an hour to climb down! After enduring too long the endless waits and crushes, management have closed the glass-encased 102nd floor to the public.

## HIGHLIGHTS

- The view: by day, at dusk and by night
- The view up from 34th Street
- New York Skyride
- Observatory Audio Tour
- Lights on the top 30 stories (➤ 12)

## INFORMATION

- ✚ E6; Locator map B2
- ✉ 350 Fifth Avenue (W34th Street)
- ☎ 212/736–3100; www.esbnyc.com
- ◉ Daily 9.30am–midnight (last admission 11.15pm)
- 🍴 Snack bar
- 🚇 B, D, F, N, Q, R, V, W34th Street
- 🚌 M1, M2, M3, M4, M5, M16, M34
- 🚉 PATH 33rd Street
- ♿ Good
- 💲 Moderate
- ↔ NY Public Library (➤ 36), Chrysler Building (➤ 37)

Top: *The view*
Below: *The entrance hall*

**11**

# New York Public Library

## INFORMATION

- ✚ E4; Locator map B2
- ✉ 476 Fifth Avenue (42nd Street)
- ☎ 212/869-8089; www.nypl.org
- 🕐 Tue–Wed 11–7.30, Thu–Sat 10–6; closed holidays
- 🍴 Kiosks outside (not winter)
- 🚇 4, 5, 6, 7, S 42nd Street Grand Central
- 🚌 M101, M102
- 🚂 Metro North, Grand Central
- ♿ Good (also see below)
- 🎟 Free
- ❓ Tours 11am and 2pm daily. Notable branches include the Andrew Heiskell Library for the Blind and Physically Handicapped (✉ 40 W20th Street) and the Library for the Performing Arts (✉ 40 Lincoln Plaza)

**Why are we sending you to a library on your vacation? Because the New York Public Library's Central Research Building is a great, white, hushed palace, beautiful to behold even if you have no time to open a book.**

**The building**  Carrère and Hastings (who also designed the Frick, ► 43) were the architects responsible for what is generally thought the city's best representative of the beaux-arts style—the sumptuous yet classical French school that flourished in New York's "gilded age," about 1880–1920. A pair of lions, which Mayor La Guardia christened Patience and Fortitude, flank the majestic stair that leads directly into the barrel-vaulted, carved white marble temple of Astor Hall. The lions are themselves flanked by fountains, "Truth" and "Beauty," which echo the site's previous (1845–99) incarnation as the Croton Reservoir supplying the city's water. Behind this briefly stood New York's version of London's Crystal Palace, built for the first American World's Fair in 1853. Like the London one, it burned down. Inside, see temporary exhibitions in the Gottesman Hall, and look up! The carved oak ceiling is sublime; read in the two-block-long Main Reading Room; see library collection rarities in the Salomon Room; and don't miss the Richard Haas murals of NYC publishing houses in the De Witt Wallace Periodical Room.

**The books**  The library owns over 15 million books, most living in the 82 branches. This building is dedicated to research. The CATNYP computer, complete with dumb waiter, can disgorge any of the 16 million manuscripts or 3 million books from the 92 miles (148km) of stacks in ten minutes flat.

## Chrysler Building

**"Which is your favorite New York building?" goes the annoying yet perennial question. Nine out of ten people who express a preference pick the Chrysler Building. This should surprise nobody who gazes on it.**

**King for a year** The tower, commissioned from William Van Alen by Walter Chrysler (who asked for something "taller than the Eiffel Tower"), won the world's tallest building competition in 1930... until the Empire State Building went up the following year. Van Alen had been almost beaten by Craig Severance's Bank of Manhattan tower at 40 Wall Street, when his rival, aware of the unofficial race, slung on an extra two feet. Unbeknownst to Severance, though, Van Alen was secretly constructing a 123-ft (37-m) stainless steel spire, which he "slotted" out through the 925-ft (282-m) roof, beating the 927-footer hands down. It is sort of ironic that the best view of the art-deco beauty's top is now gained from the observatory at the Empire State.

**Multi-story car** Every detail of the 77-story building evokes the automobile—a 1929 Chrysler Plymouth, to be exact. The winged steel gargoyles are modeled on its radiator caps; other of the building's stepped setbacks carry stylized hubcaps and the entire spire resembles a radiator grill; and this ain't no Toyota. The golden age of cars is further evoked by the stunning lobby, which you can visit—ostensibly to view the Con Edison (New York's utilities company) conservation exhibit, but really to see the red marble, granite and chrome interior, surmounted by the 97- by 100-ft (30-m by 31-m) mural depicting industrial scenes and celebrating "transportation."

### HIGHLIGHTS

- Spire
- Ceiling mural
- Elevator cabs
- Fourth setback gargoyles
- African marble lobby

### INFORMATION

- F4; Locator map B2
- 405 Lexington Avenue (42nd Street)
- Mon–Fri 7am–6pm; closed holidays
- 4, 5, 6, 7, S 42nd Street, Grand Central
- M101, M102
- Metro North, Grand Central
- Good
- Free

*The pinnacle of success*

**13**

# Grand Central Terminal

## INFORMATION

**Don't call it a station. All tracks terminate here, which makes this a far grander entity. The beaux-arts building bustles like no place else. As the saying goes—stand here long enough, and the entire world passes by.**

**Heart of the nation** "Grand Central Station!" bellowed (erroneously) the 1937 opening of the eponymous NBC radio drama; "Beneath the glitter and swank of Park Avenue… Crossroads of a million private lives!… Heart of the nation's greatest city…" And so it is, and has been since 1871 when the first, undersized version was opened by Commodore Cornelius Vanderbilt, who had bought up all the city's railroads, just like on a giant Monopoly board. See him in bronze below Jules-Alexis Coutans' allegorical statuary on the main façade (south, 42nd Street). The current building dates from 1913 and is another beaux-arts glory, its design modeled partly on the Paris Opéra by architects Warren and Wetmore. William Wilgus was the logician responsible for traffic-marshaling, while Reed & Stem were the overall engineers. Look up at the main concourse ceiling for the stunning sight of 2,500 "stars" in a cerulean sky, with medieval-style zodiac signs by French artist Paul Helleu.

**Meeting under the clock** The fame of the four-faced clock atop the information booth is out of all proportion to its size. (You may remember the scene in the movie *The Fisher King* where thousands of commuters fell into synchronized waltzing around it.) Beneath the clock, and the ground, is a warren of 32 miles (52km) of tracks, tunnels and vaulted chambers, in one the famed Oyster Bar resides. The Food Court is virtually a new neighborhood. Be careful what you say here—the acoustics are amazing.

# Rockefeller Center

**This small village of famous art-deco buildings provides many of those "Gee, this is New York" moments: especially in winter when you see ice-skaters ringed by the flags of the UN, and gaze up at the massive tree.**

Prometheus is here The buildings' bible, Willensky and White's *AIA Guide to NYC*, calls the 19-building Rockefeller Center "The greatest urban complex of the 20th century." It is "the heart of New York," agreed the Landmarks Commission in 1985. So the architectural importance of the center—and especially the elongated ziggurat GE Building (better known as the RCA Building)—is beyond dispute, but it's still easy to enjoy the place. Rest on a Channel Gardens bench, enjoy the seasonal foliage and gaze on the lower plaza, the rink and Paul Manship's *Prometheus*. The Channel is a reference to the English Channel, since these sloping gardens separate La Maison Française from the British Empire Building.

Rockefeller the Younger The realization of John D. Rockefeller Jr.'s grand scheme to outdo dad (Mister Standard Oil) provided work for a quarter of a million souls during the Depression. In 1957, Marilyn Monroe detonated the dynamite for the Time & Life building's foundations, and the Center was still growing into the 1970s.

Conan and Rockettes For many years, the NBC Studios in the GE Building hosted the hip TV talk show *Late Night* with David Letterman. Dave decamped to CBS, and the now-famous Conan O'Brian was plucked from obscurity to host the spot. Over on Avenue of the Americas is Radio City Music Hall, landmark home to the Rockettes, born in 1934 and still kicking.

Atlas, *Lee Lawrie*

## HIGHLIGHTS

- GE Building, outside
- GE Building's lobbies
- NBC Studio tour
- Skating in winter
- Sea Grill restaurant
- Radio City Music Hall
- Channel Gardens
- *Prometheus* (1934)
- Atlas (Fifth Avenue, 50th–51st streets)

## INFORMATION

- E3; Locator map B2
- Fifth–Seventh avenues (47th–52nd streets)
- 212/632–3972; www.rockefellercenter.com
- Various
- Many restaurants, cafés
- B, D, F 47th–50th streets, Rockefeller Center
- M1, M2, M3, M4, M5, M18
- Moderate
- Free
- Radio City tours 212/247–4777; NBC Studio tours 212/664–3700

39

# Museum of Modern Art

## INFORMATION

- Off Map at L1; Locator map off C1
- 45–20 33rd Street at Queens Boulevard, Long Island City
- 212/708–9400; www.moma.org
- Sat–Mon, Thu 10–5, Fri 10–7.45
- Restaurant
- #7 local 33rd Street Queens (NB the express train does not stop at MoMA)
- Q32
- Moderate

**While the midtown museum is rebuilt, the great collection has moved to Queens—now known as MoMA QNS. A roaring success, the temporary quarters have attracted a whole new crowd of art fans to the borough.**

**Van Gogh to Man Ray** Founded on the 1931 bequest of Lillie P. Bliss, which consisted of 235 works, the MoMA collections now amount to about 100,000 pieces of art. These include household objects, photography, graphic design, conceptual art and industrial design, though work from the first half of the 20th century is better represented than the really new.

**Postimpressionists to Graffiti artists** The collection starts in the late 19th century, with the Postimpressionists and Fauvists: Cézanne, Van Gogh, Monet, Manet, Pissarro, Seurat, Gauguin and Matisse. Among the 20th-century movements represented are Cubism, Futurism, Expressionism, Surrealism, Abstract Expressionism, Pop (Oldenburg, Dine, Rauschenberg and Warhol) and the "Graffiti" work of Keith Haring and Jean-Michel Basquiat.

**Viva Queens** There is much to be said for making the—none too arduous—trek on the train to MoMA QNS, and not just for the rotating selection from the painting and sculpture collections and the big exhibitions. At weekends, the free Queens Artlink shuttle connects it with the nearby exciting PS1 contemporary arts center (MoMA's affiliate since 2000), plus three more Queens' arts highlights. And admission gets you free entry to the fab film series at MoMA's Gramercy Theater back in Manhattan. Many will be disappointed when midtown reopens in 2005.

## Lincoln Center

**Strolling to the fantastically fairy-lit ten-story Metropolitan Opera House colonnade across the Central Plaza on a winter's night is one of the most glamorous things you can do on this earth, and you don't need tickets.**

**West Side Story** The ambitious Rockefeller-funded über-arts center was envisaged in the late 1950s and finished in 1969, after 7,000 families and 800 businesses had been kicked out of their homes by developer Robert Moses and the John D. Rockefeller millions. Much of *West Side Story* was actually shot on these streets after the demolition had begun, capturing the pain of change forever.

**All the arts** The 15 acres (6ha) include mega-houses for the biggest-scale arts, all designed by different architects in the same white travertine. The Metropolitan Opera House is the glamour queen, with her vast Marc Chagall murals, miles of red carpet, swooshes of stair and starry chandeliers that swiftly, silently and thrillingly rise to the sky-high gold-leafed ceiling before performances. Avery Fisher Hall caught America's oldest orchestra, the NY Philharmonic, on its trajectory out of Carnegie Hall, while the Juilliard School of Music keeps it supplied with fresh maestri. The New York State Theater, housing the New York City Opera and the New York City Ballet, faces Avery Fisher across the Plaza. Two smaller theaters, the Vivian Beaumont and Mitzi Newhouse, and a more intimate concert hall, Alice Tully, plus the Walter Reade movie theater, the little Bruno Walter Auditorium and the Guggenheim Bandshell for outdoor summer concerts, complete the pack. Over 13,500 arts fans can be swallowed simultaneously. Just don't expect to find a cab afterward.

### HIGHLIGHTS

- Chandeliers in the Met auditorium
- Reflecting Pool with Henry Moore's *Reclining Figure* (1965)
- Lincoln Center Out-of-Doors Festival
- NY City Ballet's *Nutcracker*
- Chagall murals, Met foyer
- Thursday morning rehearsals, Avery Fisher
- New York Film Festival
- Philip Johnson's Plaza fountain
- Chamber Music Society, Alice Tully
- Annual *Messiah* singalong

### INFORMATION

- a9; Locator map A1
- Broadway (62nd–67th streets)
- 212/546–2656; Met 212/362–6000; Avery Fisher 212/721–6500; www.lincolncenter.org
- Inquire for performance times
- Restaurants, cafés, bars
- 1, 9 66th Street Lincoln Center
- M5, M7, M104, crosstown M66
- Good
- Admission to Center free
- Tours leave from concourse under Met, daily 10–5
  212/875–5350

41

# Central Park

## INFORMATION

- ✚ c2–9; Locator map B1
- ☎ 212/794–6564 or 800/201–7275; www.centralparknyc.org
- ⓘ Dairy Information Center Tue–Thu, Sat–Sun 11–5, Fri 1–5
- 🍴 Restaurants, kiosks
- Ⓠ B, D, A, C Columbus Circle; 72, 81 96th Street; N, R 57th Street; B, Q 57th Street; 4, 5, 6 86th Street; 2, 3 110th Street
- 🚌 M1, M2, M3, M4, M5, M10, M18. Crosstown M66, M30, M72, M86
- ♿ Moderate
- 🎟 Free
- ↔ American Museum of Natural History (► 45)

**The park is the escape valve on the pressure cooker. Without it New York would overheat—especially in summer, when the humidity tops 90 percent, and bikers, runners, bladers, dog strollers and Frisbee players convene. It's a way of life.**

**The Greensward Plan** In the mid-19th century, when there was no Manhattan north of 42nd Street, *New York Evening Post* editor, William Cullen Bryant, campaigned until the city invested the fortune of $5million in an 840-acre (340-ha) wasteland swarming with pig-farming squatters who ran bone-boiling operations. Responsible for clearing the land was journalist Frederick Law Olmsted, who, with English architect Calvert Vaux, also won the competition to design the park, with his "Greensward Plan." By day, Olmsted supervised the shifting of 5 million cubic tons of dirt; by night, he and Vaux trod the wasteland acres and designed. Night strolls are not recommended nowadays.

**Fun and games** Start at the Dairy Information Center, and pick up a map and events list. These show the lie of the land and tell you about the Wildlife Conservation Center (Zoo), the Carousel, the playgrounds, rinks, fountains, statues and Strawberry Fields, where John Lennon is commemorated close to the Dakota Building where he lived and was shot. But the busy life of the park is not recorded on maps: showing off rollerblade moves on the Mall by the Sheep Meadow; hanging out at the Heckscher Playground and Great Lawn softball leagues; doing the loop road fast, by bike; sunbathing, poolside, at the vast Lasker Pool in Harlem; playing rowboat dodgems on the Lake; bouldering on the outcrops of Manhattan schist...

# Frick Collection

**Like the Wallace Collection in London and the Musée Picasso in Paris, Henry Clay Frick's mansion is half the reason for seeing his collection. Henry bequeathed these riches to the nation as a memorial to himself—that's the kind of guy he was.**

**The mansion, and the man**  Henry Clay Frick was chairman of the Carnegie Steel Corp. (US Steel). He was one of the most ruthless strike-breakers of all time and the nastiest industrialist of his day. Instead of any comeuppance (though there were several assassination attempts), he got to commission Carrère and Hastings (who designed the NY Public Library) to build him one of the last great beaux-arts mansions on Fifth Avenue and fill it with an exquisite collection of 14th- to 19th-century old masters, porcelain, furniture and bronzes. Not much of the furniture is velvet-roped, so you can rest in a Louis XVI chair before strolling in the central glass-roofed courtyard and the gorgeous garden.

**What Frick bought**  Some of the 40 rooms are arranged around a particular work or artist, notably the Boucher Room, east of the entrance, and the Fragonard Room, with the 11-painting *Progress of Love* series. There are British masters (Constable, Gainsborough, Whistler, Turner), Dutch (Vermeer, Rembrandt, Van Eyck, Hals), Italian (Titian, Bellini, Veronese) and Spanish (El Greco, Goya, Velázquez). Interspersed are Limoges enamel and Chinese porcelain, Persian carpets and Marie Antoinette's furniture. Some Frick descendants still have keys to this modest pied à terre, which, as well as what you see, has a bowling alley in the basement.

## HIGHLIGHTS

- *Mall in St. James' Park*, Gainsborough (1783)
- *Sir Thomas More*, Holbein (1527)
- *Officer and the Laughing Girl*, Vermeer (1655–60)
- *The Polish Rider*, Rembrandt (c1655)
- *Virgin and Child with Saints*, Van Eyck (c1441–43)
- *Philip IV of Spain*, Velázquez (1644)

## INFORMATION

- d8; Locator map B1
- 1 E70th Street
- 212/288–0700; www.frick.org
- Tue–Sat 10–6 (also Fri to 9), Sun 1–6; closed holidays
- 6 68th Street
- M1, M2, M3, M4
- Good
- Moderate
- Lectures: Wed 5.30

Virgin and Child with Saints, *Van Eyck*

# Whitney Museum of American Art

## HIGHLIGHTS

- Biennial
- *Circus*, Alexander Calder (1926–31)
- The Hoppers
- The O'Keeffes
- *Dempsey and Firpo*, George Bellows (1924)
- The Louise Nevelsons
- Drawbridge

## INFORMATION

- e7; Locator map B1
- 945 Madison Avenue (75th Street)
- 212/570–3676; www.whitney.org
- Tue–Thu, Sat–Sun 11–6, Fri 1–9; closed holidays
- Café
- 6 77th Street
- M1, M2, M3, M4
- Good
- Moderate
- Lectures, video/film: Whitney at the Philip Morris Building ⊠ Park Avenue (42nd Street) ☎ 212/663–2453 ◑ Mon–Fri 11–6; closed holidays

**More modern than the Modern, the Whitney wants to be as unpredictable as the *artist du jour*, and very often succeeds. It's a New York tradition to sneer at the Biennial, whether or not one has seen the show.**

**No room at the Met**  Sculptor and patron of her contemporaries' work, Gertrude Vanderbilt Whitney offered her collection to the Met in 1929, but the great institution turned up its nose, and Whitney was forced to found the Whitney. In 1966, Marcel Breuer's cantilevered, granite-clad Brutalist block was completed to house it in suitably controversial manner, and here it lours still, not universally loved, but impossible to overlook. The Whitney's core collection now reads like a roll call of American (and immigrant) 20th-century greats: Edward Hopper, Thomas Hart Benton, Willem de Kooning, Georgia O'Keeffe, Claes Oldenburg, Jasper Johns, George Bellows, Jackson Pollock are a few (the male to female ratio has improved, but barely). Let's hope the curators and buyers are as good as Gertrude at spotting talent for the future. There are so many more artists these days…

**Take your pick**  Exhibitions, drawn from the museum's important and delicious collection, often emphasize a single artist's work. At other times they prove more eclectic. There's an active film and video department, and a branch in Park Avenue. There used to be four branches in Manhattan alone during the art boomtime of the 1980s. The Whitney Biennial (in the spring of even-numbered years) provides an echo of those days, when the New York art pack gets sweaty debating the merits and demerits of the chosen few on show and of the curator's vision—for the Biennial is invitational, and makes careers.

# American Museum of Natural History

**No longer a lovable anachronism since its renovation, this 19th-century hulk is stuffed with dinosaur skeletons and appended by the amazing Rose Center. The blue whale's cocktail bar and the dioramas are delightful.**

**Who's who**   Of the 36 million things owned by the museum—which is, needless to say, the largest such institution in the world—only a small percentage is on show. Among the improvements funded by a $45-million cash injection were a sprucing-up of the buildings themselves, and, most notably, the metamorphosed Hayden Planetarium, now the Rose Center, next door, with its thrill ride through the universe (accompanied by Tom Hanks). Another highlight is the partially interactive dinosaurs to please computer-jaded children. There's far too much to see in one day, with three city blocks and the entire evolution of life on earth covered. Not-to-be-missed items include the barosaurus rearing up to her full 55ft (17m) to protect her young from a T-rex attack; and the 94-ft (29-m) blue whale that dominates the two-story Hall of Ocean Life and Biology of Fishes and presides over its own bar.

**More gems**   Another highlight is the 563-carat Star of India sapphire, part of the unbelievable Hall of Meteorites, Minerals and Gems, containing almost $50-million worth of precious stones, plus the 34-ton Ahnighito meteorite. The cutest part of the museum is where animals of all sizes are displayed behind glass in *tableaux morts* of considerable artistic merit. In the Nature Max theater a four-story screen shows ecological blockbusters, but it's the new planetarium, a dramatic 87-ft (27-m) sphere in a glass cube, with its Friday night jazz-and-tapas, that takes the cake.

## HIGHLIGHTS

- Blue whale
- Barosaurus
- Herd of stuffed elephants
- New dinosaur halls
- Sky Shows
- Star of India
- The dioramas
- Dinosaur embryo
- "Starry Nights" jazz at the Rose

## INFORMATION

- ✚ b6; Locator map B1
- ✉ Central Park West (79th Street)
- ☎ 212/769–5100; www.amnh.org
- 🕐 Daily 10–5.45
- 🍽 Various
- Ⓜ B, C 81st Street
- 🚌 M7, M10, M11, M79
- ♿ Good
- 💲 Moderate to expensive
- 🔗 Lincoln Center (➤ 41), Central Park (➤ 42)
- ❓ 75-minute tours until 3.15. Rose Center ☎ 212/769–5200

*The barosaurus*

45

# Metropolitan Museum of Art

## HIGHLIGHTS

- Temple of Dendur (15BC)
- Period rooms, American Wing
- *Young Woman with a Water Jug*, Vermeer (1660–67)
- *Venus and Adonis*, Rubens (1630s)
- *Grand Canal, Venice*, Turner (c 1835)

*The Great Hall*

## INFORMATION

- ✚ d6; Locator map B1
- ✉ 1000 Fifth Avenue (82nd Street)
- ☎ 212/535–7710; www.metmuseum.org
- 🕐 Tue–Thu, Sun 9.30–5.15, Fri, Sat 9.30–8.45
- 🍴 Cafeteria, restaurant, bar
- Ⓔ 4, 5, 6 86th Street
- 🚌 M1, M2, M3, M4
- ♿ Good
- 💵 Moderate
- ↔ Central Park (➤ 42), Whitney (➤ 44),
- ❓ The Cloisters (➤ 50) houses more of the Met's medieval collections; same-day admission on Met ticket

**It will give you bigger blisters than the Uffizi, bigger chills than the Sistine Chapel and take a bigger slice of vacation time than all dinners. It's so big, it doesn't just contain Egyptian artifacts, but an entire Egyptian building.**

**Art city**   The limestone beaux-arts façade with its tremendous steps was a 1902 addition to the Calvert Vaux (of Central Park fame) red-brick Gothic building buried inside here. There are several more buildings-within-buildings, interior gardens and courtyards, such is the scale of the Met. The 15BC Temple of Dendur, in its glass-walled bemoated chamber east of the main entrance on the upper floor, is the best known, but there's much more besides: the Astor Court above it—a replica Ming dynasty scholar's courtyard—plus, in the American Wing, a score of period-style rooms, and the vast and sunlit garden court with its hodgepodge of Tiffany glass and topiary, a Frank Lloyd Wright window and the entire Federal-style façade of the United States Bank from Wall Street.

**Where to start? How to stop?**   A quarter of the 3 million-plus objects are up at any one time, so pace yourself. Relax. There are about 15 discrete collections. Some visitors decide on one or two per visit—13th- to 18th-century European Paintings (or part thereof) and Ancient Art, perhaps—and leave it at that. Or you could structure a route around one or two favorite and familiar works. On the gound level, the Information Center in the Uris Center, with its Orientation Theater and giant floor plans, is the place to begin, whatever you decide to see. Consider visiting on Friday or Saturday evening, when a string quartet serenades you, and there are far fewer crowds.

# Solomon R. Guggenheim Museum

**If you just happened across Frank Lloyd Wright's space-age rotunda, your eyes would pop out of their sockets, but it's the planet's best-known modern building, so you are prepared. Don't forget the art inside.**

**Museum of architecture**  This is the great Frank Lloyd Wright's only New York building, his "Pantheon," as he called it. It was commissioned by Solomon R. Guggenheim at the urging of his friend and taste tutor, Baroness Hilla Rebay von Ehrenwiesen, though the wealthy metal-mining magnate died ten years before it was completed in 1959. The giant white nautilus is certainly arresting, but it's the interior that unleashes the most superlatives. Take the elevator to the top level and snake your way down the museum's spiral ramp to see why. You can study the exhibits, look over the parapet to the lobby below, and finish up where you began without ever losing your way.

**Museum of art**  There are around 6,000 pieces in the Guggenheim Foundation's possession. Solomon R. and his wife Irene Rothschild abandoned the Old Masters they sought at first, when Hilla Rebay introduced them to Léger, Kandinsky, Mondrian and Moholy-Nagy, Chagall and Gleizes, and they got hooked on the moderns. See also the early Picassos in the small rotunda and the 1992 tower extension. If you like the Impressionists and Postimpressionists, look for the Thannhauser Collection, donated to the museum by art dealer Joseph K. Thannhauser and always on display—unlike the Guggenheim holdings, which are rotated. A spectacular new Guggenheim museum, designed by Frank Gehry, is being planned for Piers 9, 11, 13, and 14 on the East River, Lower Manhattan.

## HIGHLIGHTS

- The building
- *l'Hermitage à Pontoise*, Pissarro (1867)
- *Paris Through the Window*, Chagall (1913)
- *Woman Ironing*, Picasso (1904)
- *Nude*, Modigliani (1917)
- Kandinskys
- Klees
- Légers
- The store

## INFORMATION

- d5; Locator map E4
- 1071 Fifth Avenue (88th Street)
- 212/423–3500; www.guggenheim. org/new_york
- Sat–Wed 10–6, Fri 10–8; closed 25 Dec, 1 Jan
- Café
- 4, 5, 6 86th Street
- M1, M2, M3, M4
- Good
- Moderate
- Central Park (► 42), Whitney Museum of American Art (► 44), Metropolitan Museum of Art (► 46)
- Lecture program

47

# Cooper-Hewitt Design Museum

## HIGHLIGHTS

- Paneling in the hall
- Solarium
- Garden
- Architectural drawings
- Summer concerts
- Textiles
- Exhibitions

## INFORMATION

- ✚ d4; Locator map E4
- ✉ 2 E91st Street
- ☎ 212/849–8300;
  www.ndm.si.edu
- 🕐 Tue 10–9, Wed–Fri 10–5,
  Sat 10–6, Sun noon–6;
  closed holidays
- 🍴 None
- Ⓜ 4, 5, 6 86th Street
- 🚌 M1, M2, M3, M4
- ♿ Good
- 💲 Inexpensive
- ↔ Central Park (► 42),
  Guggenheim (► 47)
- ❓ Tours available

**The charming Cooper-Hewitt Design Museum collections are exhibited in an elegant, wood-paneled mansion. When snow falls in the holiday season, there's nowhere better to indulge in mawkishly nostalgic reveries.**

**Carnegie-Hewitt** The mansion belonged to industrialist Andrew Carnegie, who, in 1903, had asked architects Babb, Cook & Willard for "the most modest, plainest and most roomy house in New York City." This he did not receive (aside from the roominess), since this little château was built with modern conveniences galore—air conditioning and elevators—and a big gated garden to keep out the squatter neighbors. The entire neighborhood came to be known as Carnegie Hill, thanks to his early patronage. Andrew's wife, Louise, lived here till her death in 1946, then, some 20 years later, the Carnegie Corporation donated it to the Smithsonian Institution to house the Hewitt sisters' collections. Still following? The three sisters, Amy, Eleanor and Sarah, had become infatuated with London's museums in 1897, and this set them off on their lifelong collecting spree.

**And Cooper** The girls' grandpa was Peter Cooper, founder of the Cooper Union college of art and architecture, and he offered the collection a home there, where it stayed until 1967. The contemporary Cooper-Hewitt is a vibrant institution where all kinds of event are happening. In addition to the collections, some of which are on display (though it's hard to predict which), there are various reference resources, including the country's biggest architectural drawings collection, a textile library with a 3,000-year span, auction catalogs, wallpapers, jewelry, earthenware—you name it.

Top: *The former residence of the industrialist Andrew Carnegie and home to the Cooper-Hewitt Museum*

# Yankee Stadium

**Final out, bottom of the ninth and, whether the home team has won or lost, Sinatra's "New York, New York" wafts over the blue seats. Baseball embodies the American spirit: this stadium is New York.**

**What baseball means**  New Yorkers are sports mad, even though a team nowadays is more a brand name than a group of athletes. Professional baseball today is a big-bucks business, which reached its apogee of heartlessness with the players' strike of 1994. To Yankee fans that bad year was eclipsed by their team's incredible winning streak—after clinching the 1996, 1998 and 1999 World Series titles, the Yanks won the first "Subway Series" (so called because NYC Transit runs between the stadiums) since 1956.

**The house that Ruth built**  If you want to see what makes the New Yorker tick (unless they're fans of the National League NY Mets), go see a Yankees home game. The Yankees dominated the early eras of baseball. In 1920 Babe Ruth joined the team and quickly became a hero of such mythic stature that his popularity built them a stadium in 1923 (renovated in the mid-1970s).

**Where have you gone, Joe Di Maggio?**  The Babe's No. 3 is only one of the "retired" numbers that honor great players who bore them and that will never be re-allocated. Lou Gehrig was No. 4; No. 5 was Joe Di Maggio (he who married Marilyn Monroe and pulled off a 56-game hitting streak); No. 7 was Mickey Mantle and No. 8 was Yogi Berra. These four played between 1946 and 1960, when the team won eight World Series titles—a record that may yet be broken.

## HIGHLIGHTS

- The 2000 Subway Series
- Bleachers (inexpensive seats)
- The groundsmen's YMCA diamond-sweeping
- Eddie Layton, organist
- "Giveaway Days"

## INFORMATION

- Off map; Locator map E2
- E161st Street, Bronx
- 718/293–4300; Ticketmaster 212/307–1212; www.yankees.com
- Season runs Apr–Oct. Check schedule for games
- Concession stands
- 4, B, D 161st Street
- BX6, BX13, BX55
- Good
- Expensive

49

# The Cloisters

## INFORMATION

- Off map; Locator map D1
- Fort Tryon Park, North Manhattan
- 718/923–3700; www.metmuseum.org/collections
- Tue–Sun 9.30–5.15, Mar–Oct; Tue–Sun 9.30–4.45, rest of year. Closed holidays
- A 190th Street
- M4
- Good
- Moderate
- Tours Tue–Fri 3, Sun noon. Joint same-day admission with the Met. Concert program of live and recorded medieval music

**A 12th-century Spanish apse attached to a Romanesque cloister and a Gothic chapel—what's all this doing in the Bronx? This is the Met's medieval branch: the incongruity is hallucinogenic, and amazing enough in itself, but the sights are just heavenly.**

**Medieval world**  The building in Fort Tryon Park—a site in the far north of Manhattan Island that was donated by Rockefeller Jr.—is not medieval, you'll be astonished to learn, but there are plenty of parts of buildings inside it that are. The 12th-century pink stone Cuxa Cloister was liberated from the French Pyrenees, and the 3,000 limestone blocks of the Fuentidueña Chapel apse were rescued from the ruins of the church of Saint-Martín in Spain. The Cloisters are not some Disney-esque simulacrum of medieval Europe, however. Being able to gaze at the ribbed vaulting of the late-Romanesque Pontaut Chapter House, or strolling past the early-Flemish Annunciation Altarpiece of Robert Campin to the familiar 15th-century Unicorn Tapestries, are treats that have not been possible in Europe since the Age of Chivalry exhibition at London's Royal Academy gathered together high points of medieval art some years ago.

**Through the ages**  The collections are arranged chronologically, so you can trace not only the metamorphosis of architectural styles, but also of the medieval mind—by turns awestruck, playful, bawdy and terrified. The bulk of the art and architecture was amassed by sculptor George Gray Bernard in the early 20th century. Much was rescued from ruin: the effigy of the Crusader Jean d'Alluye, for instance, was doing duty as a bridge, while the priceless Unicorn Tapestries were once draped over trees as frost blankets.

# NEW YORK CITY's
# best

# Buildings

### R.I.P. TWIN TOWERS

The 110-story towers of the World Trade Center, a quarter of a mile tall, were struck at 8.48am (north tower) and 9.03am (south tower) on that incongruously sunny day in September 2001. They took roughly 12 seconds each to crumple, the south tower at 9.59am, the north at 10.28am (a stone dropped from one would have taken 9.2 seconds to reach the ground). An estimated 3,000 lives were lost in by far the worst tragedy ever to have hit New York. The impact on many financial institutions was also great, since the towers housed 50,000 workers in 218 acres (88ha) of office space. Reconstruction of the area will continue for years, but nobody will ever forget what the city lost.

*Before 11 September the Lower Manhattan skyline was dominated by the twin towers*

### CATHEDRAL OF ST. JOHN THE DIVINE

Started in 1892 and not finished yet, this would be the world's biggest.
🔳 a1 ✉ Amsterdam Avenue (W112th Street) ☎ 212/316–7540
🕐 Mon–Sat 7–5, Sun 7am–8pm 🚇 1, 9 110th Street

### CITICORP CENTER

The 45-degree lightbox is one of the skyline's greatest hits at night. The four-legged base shelters St. Peter's Church and the great atrium.
🔳 F2 ✉ 153 E53rd Street 🚇 6 51st Street

### THE DAKOTA

First of the great Upper West Side luxury apartment houses, designed by Henry Hardenberg, but famous as John Lennon's murder site.
🔳 b7 ✉ 1 W72nd Street (Central Park West) 🚇 B, C 72nd Street

### FLATIRON BUILDING

This 1902 skyscraper was named after its amazing shape: an isosceles triangle with a sharp angle pointing uptown.

➕ E8 ✉ 175 Fifth Avenue (E22nd/23rd streets) 🚇 N, R 23rd Street

### GRACIE MANSION

Gracie Mansion has been the mayor's official residence since 1942. When it was built in 1799, this was a remote country house.

➕ Off map ✉ East End Avenue (88th Street) 🚇 4, 5, 6 86th Street

### LEVER HOUSE

The Seagram and this 1952 Skidmore, Owings & Merrill building were precursors of all glass blocks.

➕ F2 ✉ 390 Park Avenue (53rd/54th streets) ☎ 212/960–4685 🕐 Lobby Mon–Fri 10–5, Sun 1–5 🚇 E, F Fifth Avenue

### "LIPSTICK BUILDING"

This likeable 1986 show-off is by John Burgee with Philip Johnson.

➕ G2 ✉ 885 Third Avenue (55th/56th streets) 🚇 6 51st Street

### METLIFE BUILDING

Formerly known as the Pan Am Building—which it was until 1981—it's by Bauhaus priest Walter Gropius, plus Emery Roth & Sons and Pietro Belluschi.

➕ F4 ✉ 200 Park Avenue (44th–45th streets) 🚇 4, 5, 6, 7 42nd Street

### NY STOCK EXCHANGE

The neoclassical façade dates only from 1903. See trading from the gallery and recall the Crash of 1929.

➕ F17 ✉ 20 Broad Street ☎ 212/656–5167 🕐 Mon–Fri 9.15–4 🚇 2, 3, 4, 5 Wall Street; J, M, Z Broad Street 🎟 Free

### SEAGRAM BUILDING

Mies van der Rohe's 1958 bronze glazed tower is *the* Modernist landmark. Philip Johnson interiors.

➕ F2 ✉ 375 Park Avenue (52nd/53rd streets) ☎ 212/572–7000 🕐 Tour Tue 3pm 🍴 Two 🚇 E, F Fifth Avenue 🎟 Free

### TRUMP TOWER

"Glitzy" captured in pink marble and glass.

➕ E1 ✉ 725 Fifth Avenue (56th Street) ☎ 212/832–2000 🕐 8am–10pm 🍴 Several 🚇 E, F Fifth Avenue

### UNITED NATIONS HEADQUARTERS

Officially outside the US, this vast 1947–63 complex included Le Corbusier among its architects.

➕ H3 ✉ First Avenue (45th Street) ☎ 212/963–7713 🕐 Fri–Wed 9.15–4.45; closed weekends Jan–Feb, 1 Jan, 25 Dec 🍴 Café and restaurant 🚇 4, 5, 6, 7 42nd Street, Grand Central 🎟 Free

*The Flatiron Building was one of the first structures to be erected around a steel frame—the basic support of every subsequent skyscraper*

53

# Of the Old

*St. Patrick's Cathedral*

### LITERARY NEW YORK

*Old New York* is the title of a collection of Edith Wharton novellas that brings to life the *Age of Innocence* (the Wharton novel filmed by Scorsese). The other chronicler of 19th-century New York manners was, of course, Henry James, especially in *Washington Square* (filmed as *The Heiress*). For the jazz age of the 1920s, read F. Scott Fitzgerald's short stories.

### BLOCK BEAUTIFUL

This picturesque, tree-lined 1920s row really is called this. Also see the pretty square nearby, centered on private Gramercy Park (➤ 56).
➕ F8 ✉ E19th Street (Irving Place/Third Avenue) 🚇 N, R 14th Street Union Square; 6 23rd Street

### CITY HALL

French Renaissance-style façade and elegant Georgian interior—see it by visiting the Governor's Room, with a small furniture museum.
➕ F15 ✉ Broadway (Murray Street) ☎ 212/788–3000 🕐 Mon–Fri 10–3.30 🚇 2, 3 Park Place; 4, 5, 6 Brooklyn Bridge/City Hall; N, R City Hall 🎟 Free

### ST. PATRICK'S CATHEDRAL

James Renwick's Gothic Revival cathedral is the US's biggest for Catholics.
➕ E2 ✉ Fifth Avenue (50th Street) ☎ 212/753–2261 🕐 6am–9pm 🚇 6 51st Street; E, F Fifth Avenue

### SINGER BUILDING & HAUGHWOUT STORE

Two of the best ambassadors for the SoHo Cast Iron Historic District (➤ 56)—the 26 blocks of skyscraper forerunners, now galleries and upscale boutiques. The Haughwout had the first Otis steam elevator.
➕ F12 ✉ Singer: 561 Broadway. Haughwout: 488 Broadway 🚇 N, R Prince Street; F, S Broadway/Lafayette

### WASHINGTON SQUARE: "THE ROW" AND ARCH

"The Row" (1–13 north side) housed movers and shakers of early 19th-century New York City—read Henry James' *Washington Square* for details.
➕ E11 ✉ South end of Fifth Avenue 🚇 N, R 8th Street; A, C, E, B, D, F, Q W4th Street

### WOOLWORTH BUILDING

The world's tallest until the Chrysler, Cass Gilbert's Gothic beauty has NYC's richest lobby—see the witty bas reliefs of Gilbert and tycoon F. W. Woolworth.
➕ F16 ✉ 233 Broadway 🕐 Lobby Mon–Fri 7–6; closed holidays 🚇 2, 3 Park Place; N, R City Hall

# Views

### A TABLE WITH A VIEW

This is a sought-after commodity. Eat well (and pay handsome sums) at Brooklyn's River Café (✉ 1 Water Street ☎ 718/522–5200) or the Water's Edge in Queens (✉ 44th Drive, East River, Long Island City ☎ 718/482–0033), with its free boat taxi and floor-to-ceiling windows. The Water Club (✉ 500 E30th Street ☎ 212/683–3333) has the view in the other direction, and new American food. Or dine waterside at the Boathouse Café (☎ 212/517–2233) on Central Park's lake.

### BROOKLYN HEIGHTS PROMENADE

As traffic clogs the Brooklyn–Queens Expressway beneath your feet, all is serene on this elegantissimo promenade, with some of New York's most covetable houses and rare gardens at your back, and the view of Lower Manhattan (with its sad gap) spread out before you.

✚ J18 ✉ West end of Clark Street 🚇 2, 3 Clark Street

### PARK AVENUE FROM CARNEGIE HILL

The view from here to the MetLife building is best experienced during the Christmas holiday season when pine trees bedecked with sparkling white lights bisect the route.

✚ e4–5 🚇 6 86th Street, 96th Street

### ROOSEVELT ISLAND TRAMWAY

One of New York City's oddities is this Swiss-made cable car that has been flying passengers to the site of the NYC. Lunatic Asylum (undergoing restoration) and on into Queens since 1976.

✚ G1 ✉ Second Avenue (60th Street) ☎ 212/832–4543 🕐 Mon–Fri 6am–2am, Sat–Sun 6am–3am 🚇 B, Q Lexington Avenue 💲 Inexpensive

### STATEN ISLAND FERRY

Those three words "Staten Island Ferry" are nearly always followed by these three: "city's best bargain." The voyage is a tiny vacation.

✚ F19 ✉ Whitehall Terminal ☎ 212/806–6901 or 718/390–5253 🕐 24-hour service 🚇 4 Bowling Green 💲 Free

### BATTERY PARK CITY

Watch the sunset on the Hudson from a bench in the gardens here.

✚ D16–D18 🚇 4 Bowling Green

*See New York from above, on the Roosevelt Island Tramway*

# Neighborhoods

**EAST VILLAGE**

Not long ago this was less a neighborhood, more a state of mind—the one that parents hope is just a phase. Now Houston to 14th, Third Avenue to C has been thoroughly tamed by outrageous property prices. The streets themselves are bursting with inexpensive and good restaurants, divey bars, coffee lounges, vintage clothing stores and wholefood emporia. Pretty Tompkins Square Park has great concerts in summer.

*St. Mark's Place,
East Village*

## EAST VILLAGE
What used to be the edgiest "nabe" in town is now a youthful playground of restaurants and boutiques.
➕ G10–H10 🚇 F Second Avenue; 6 Astor Place

## GRAMERCY PARK AND FLATIRON
The former—peaceful and pleasant to stroll—is centered on the eponymous park; the latter on the eponymous building (► 53). It's grown out of the photography district, and now contains "Silicon Alley" plus the Restaurant Row on Park Avenue South.
➕ E8–F8 🚇 N, R, 6 23rd Street

## LITTLE ITALY
Reduced to Mulberry Street, this is a nice place to stroll and café hop. Skip the touristy red-sauce spaghetterias, and see Scorsese's *Mean Streets* for the real thing. Adjacent streets contain extremely fashionable stores and have been dubbed "Nolita"—North of Little Italy.
➕ G13 🚇 6 Spring Street

## LOWER EAST SIDE
Where the melting pot landed; birth of Jewish New York: Orchard Street.
➕ H12–H13 🚇 F Delancey Street

## SOHO
South of Houston (say "*How*-stun") saw 1980s art mania, when its gorgeous cast-iron framed buildings were "loft-ized" on the cheap. Now it's for Chanel, Prada and chain-store shopping, plus a little remaining gallery-hopping.
➕ F13 🚇 N, R Prince Street; C, E Spring Street

## THEATER DISTRICT
As it sounds. It is delineated more or less by Sixth and Ninth avenues and 34th to 59th streets, with theaters clustering mostly on Broadway.
➕ C3/4–D3/4 🚇 N, R, 1, 2, 3 Times Square

## TRIBECA
Like SoHo, the Flatiron and the East Village, the "Triangle Below Canal" was designated a neighborhood by real estate agents, but the sobriquet stuck. Once a windy wasteland of warehouses, now it has many top tables (Montrachet, Nobu, Chanterelle), plus rich architects, artists and movie-makers in lofts.
➕ D15–E15 🚇 A, 1, 2, 3 Chambers Street

# Museums

---

**In the Top 25**

---

## JEWISH MUSEUM

The largest Jewish museum in the Western hemisphere chronicling Jewish experience worldwide, with artifacts from 4,000 years ago.
➕ d4 ✉ 1109 Fifth Avenue ☎ 212/423–3200 🕐 Sun–Thu 11–5.45, Thu 11–8, Fri 11–3 🍴 Café 🚇 4, 5, 6 86th Street
💲 Inexpensive

## LOWER EAST SIDE TENEMENT MUSEUM

This reconstruction of life in a 1863 tenement block is a must for history buffs. Well informed staff conduct intriguing tours and talks.
➕ H13 ✉ 90 Orchard Street ☎ 212/431–0233
🕐 Tue–Fri 1–3.30, Sat–Sun 11–4.30 🚇 F, J, M, Z Delancey Street; B, D, Q Grand Street 💲 Moderate

## MUSEUM OF THE CITY OF NEW YORK

Rotating exhibitions that illustrate the changing life of the city dating back to 1624. Special walking tours available.
➕ d2 ✉ 1220 Fifth Avenue (103rd Street)
☎ 212/534–1672 🕐 Wed–Sat 10–5, Sun noon–5 🚇 6 103rd Street 💲 Free (contribution)

## NEUE GALERIE NEW YORK

Early 20th-century German and Austrian art.
➕ d5 ✉ 1048 Fifth Avenue (86th Street) ☎ 212/628–6200
🕐 Fri, Sat, Mon 11–7, Sun 1–6 🚇 4, 5, 6 86th Street 💲 Moderate

## NEW MUSEUM OF CONTEMPORARY ART

What MoMA stops at, Whitney shows; where Whitney balks, this museum starts.
➕ F12 ✉ 583 Broadway (Houston/Prince streets)
☎ 212/219–1222 🕐 Wed–Sun noon–6, Sat noon–8 🚇 N, R Prince Street 💲 Inexpensive

## NEW YORK CITY FIRE MUSEUM

The intriguing story of the city's fires and those who tried to put them out, with a collection of horse-drawn carriages, ladders, photos and New York's first fire bell.
➕ D13 ✉ 278 Spring Street, SoHo ☎ 212/691–1303
🕐 Tue–Sat 10–4 🚇 C, E Spring Street 💲 Contribution

---

### MUSICAL SOIRÉES

At major museums this is an innovation catching on quickly. The Metropolitan Museum of Art started the whole thing, and among those to have jumped on the bandwagon are the Guggenheim, with jazz in Frank Lloyd Wright's rotunda; the Metropolitan's Cloisters outpost; The Rose Center for Earth and Space, with Friday jazz; and the Frick, with chamber music in its beautiful courtyard.

*New York City Fire Museum*

# Galleries & Outdoor Art

*The Phyllis Kind Gallery, SoHo*

## OUTSIDE ART

Save time and combine art with sightseeing.
*Gay Liberation* (1980), George Segal
➕ D11 ✉ Christopher Park, Sheridan Square
*Prometheus* (1934), Paul Manship
➕ E2 ✉ Rockefeller Center
*Single Form* (1964), Barbara Hepworth
➕ H3 ✉ Pool of Secretariat Building, UN, First Avenue (46th Street)
*Reclining Figure* (1965), Henry Moore
➕ a9 ✉ Reflecting Pool, Lincoln Center
*Night Presence IV* (1972), Louise Nevelson
➕ e4 ✉ Park Avenue (92nd Street)

## ART CRAWL

Doing the Chelsea Crawl and/or the few remaining SoHo galleries, with brunch and shopping (in SoHo), is one version of the quintessential New York Saturday. The following galleries are worth a look. Call for showing times (generally Tue–Sat 11–6).
🚇 Chelsea: C, E, 23rd Street. SoHo: N, R Prince Street; C, E Spring Street

## SOHO GALLERIES

| | | |
|---|---|---|
| Artists Space | ✉ 38 Greene Street | ☎ 212/226–3970 |
| Deitch Projects | ✉ 18 Wooster Street | ☎ 212/343–7300 |
| The Drawing Center | ✉ 35 Wooster Street | ☎ 212/219–2166 |

## CHELSEA GALLERIES

The new art district is way west.

| | | |
|---|---|---|
| Dia Center for the Arts | ✉ 548 W22nd Street | ☎ 212/989–5566 |
| Gagosian | ✉ 555 W24th Street | ☎ 212/741–1111 |
| Greene Naftali | ✉ 526 W26th Street | ☎ 212/463–7770 |
| Lehman Maupin | ✉ 540 W26th Street | ☎ 212/255–2923 |
| Marianne Boesky | ✉ 535 W22nd Street | ☎ 212/741–0963 |
| Marks | ✉ 522 W22nd Street | ☎ 212/243–1650 |
| Paula Cooper | ✉ 534 W21st Street | ☎ 212/255–1105 |
| Sonnabend | ✉ 536 W22nd Street | ☎ 212/627–1018 |
| White Box | ✉ 525 W26th Street | ☎ 212/714–2347 |
| White Columns | ✉ 320 W13th Street | ☎ 212/924–4212 |

## UPTOWN GALLERIES

Dressier than Chelsea or SoHo viewing.

| | | |
|---|---|---|
| ICP | ✉ 1133 Sixth Avenue | ☎ 212/857–0000 |
| Mary Boone | ✉ 745 Fifth Avenue | ☎ 212/752–2929 |
| Pace Wildenstein | ✉ 32 E57th Street | ☎ 212/421–3292 |
| Zwirner & Wirth | ✉ 32 E69th Street | ☎ 212/517–8677 |

# For Kids

---

**In the Top 25**

---

**BRONX ZOO**

The biggest city zoo in the US, 100 years old in 1999, has 4,000 animals, a kid's zoo and monorail. Don't miss the newest attraction, the $43 million Congo Gorilla Forest.

✚ Off map  ✉ Fordham Road (Bronx River Parkway Northeast)  ☎ 718/367–1010  🕐 Daily 10–5, Apr–Oct; 10–4.30, rest of year  🍴 Restaurant  🚇 2, 5 Pelham Parkway  💷 Moderate

**BROOKLYN CHILDREN'S MUSEUM**

The world's first museum for kids, founded in 1899, has tons to do, including NYC highlights in miniature and the "Totally Tots" toddler stamping ground.

✚ Off map  ✉ 145 Brooklyn Avenue, Crown Heights  ☎ 718/735–4400  🕐 Wed–Fri 2–5, Sat–Sun 10–5  🚇 C Kingston Avenue  💷 Contribution

**CHILDREN'S MUSEUM OF THE ARTS**

Highlights include the Monet Ballpond, Architects Alley and the Wonder Theater.

✚ F13  ✉ 182 Lafayette Street  ☎ 212/272–0986  🕐 Thu–Sun noon–5, Wed noon–7  🚇 6 Spring Street  💷 Inexpensive

**CHILDREN'S MUSEUM OF MANHATTAN**

Ignore the word "museum"—here they can make their own TV show.

✚ a6  ✉ 212 W83rd Street  ☎ 212/721–1223  🕐 Wed–Sun 10–5, Jun–Aug, Wed; Thu 1.30–5.30, Fri–Sun 10–5, rest of year  🚇 1, 9, B, C 86th Street  💷 Inexpensive

**FAO SCHWARZ**

The world's most famous toystore—see the movie *Big*; set advance spending and time limits. The giant singing clock at the entrance is scary.

✚ F1  ✉ 767 Fifth Avenue  ☎ 212/644–9400  🕐 Mon–Sat 9–9, Sun 10–8  🚇 E, F Fifth Avenue; 4, 6 59th Street  💷 Free

**STATEN ISLAND CHILDREN'S MUSEUM**

It is a bit of a trek, but there is always something going on here.

✚ Off map  ✉ Snug Harbor, 1000 Richmond Terrace, Staten Island  ☎ 718/273–2060  🕐 Tue–Sun noon–5  🚇 Ferry to Staten Island, then S40 bus  💷 Moderate

**KIDS' BROADWAY**

The following shows are especially suitable for youngsters:

**Beauty and the Beast**
Lunt-Fontanne
✉ 205 W46th Street
(Broadway/Eighth Avenue)
☎ 212/307–4747

**The Lion King**
New Amsterdam
✉ 214 W42nd Street
(Seventh/Eighth avenues)
☎ 212/307–4747

**Oklahoma!**
Gerschwin
✉ 222 W51st Street
☎ 212/307–4100

# What's Free

┌─ In the Top 25 ───────────────────┐
🔟 **CENTRAL PARK (▶ 42)**
🔢 **COOPER-HEWITT (TUE EVENING FREE, ▶ 48)**
🔢 **FULTON FISH MARKET, SOUTH STREET
   SEAPORT (▶ 29)**
🔢 **GUGGENHEIM
   (FRI 6–8pm PAY-WHAT-YOU-WISH, ▶ 47)**
🔢 **WHITNEY MUSEUM OF AMERICAN ART
   (FRI 6–9pm PAY-WHAT-YOU-WISH, ▶ 44)**
🔢 **NEW YORK PUBLIC LIBRARY (▶ 36)**
└───────────────────────────────────┘

## ON PARADE

New York loves a parade, and nobody does it more often than New Yorkers.

**St. Patrick's Day Parade**
✉ Fifth Avenue (44th–86th streets) 🕐 17 Mar

**Easter Parade** ✉ Fifth Avenue (44th–59th streets) 🕐 Easter Sun

**Lesbian and Gay Pride Day Parade** ✉ Fifth Avenue (Columbus Circle–Washington Square) 🕐 Late June

**Columbus Day Parade** ✉ Fifth Avenue (44th–86th Streets) 🕐 12 Oct

*Street entertainment: a sound return for a small investment*

**Halloween Parade** ✉ Greenwich Village 🕐 31 Oct

**Macy's Thanksgiving Day Parade** ✉ Central Park West (79th Street)–Broadway (34th Street) 🕐 Fourth Thu in Nov

## BEING ON TV

Write in advance for free tickets to talk shows.
✉ NBC, 30 Rockefeller Plaza ☎ 212/664–3056 🚇 B, D, F 47th–50th streets

## BIG APPLE GREETERS

Volunteers who enjoy showing off their city will take you places in New York free of charge; 48 hours' notice required.
☎ 212/669–2896

## BRYANT PARK

A patch of greenery behind the New York Public Library where summer evening "walk in" movies are a new tradition; also concerts.
➕ E4 🚇 B, D, F 42nd Street

## FORBES MAGAZINE GALLERIES

Malcolm Forbes' collections of Fabergé eggs, toy soldiers, presidential manuscripts and art.
➕ E10 ✉ 60 Fifth Avenue (12th Street)
☎ 212/206–5548 🕐 Tue–Wed, Fri–Sat 10–4 🚇 N, Q, R, W, 4, 5, 6 Union Square

## NY STOCK EXCHANGE GALLERY (▶ 53)

## SOHO AND CHELSEA GALLERY-HOPPING (▶ 58)

## STATEN ISLAND FERRY (▶ 55)

## WALKING

The world's best walking city. You'll need around two minutes per block, comfortable shoes and sunglasses.

## WASHINGTON SQUARE (▶ 54)

In summer it's live theater—literally. Genuinely funny stand-ups perform.

## PROSPECT PARK BANDSHELL (▶ 30)

Music and film, all summer long.

# Gyms

### CHELSEA PIERS SPORTS CENTER
Egalitarian, vast, packed with a four-tier golf range, two ice-skating rinks, marina, climbing wall, track and field arena and big swimming pool.

✚ A8 ✉ Piers 59–62 West Side Highway ☎ 212/336–6666
🚇 C, E 23rd Street

### CRUNCH
Cyberpunk styling, gimmicks (live DJs, haircutting, heart-rate monitors).

✚ F9 ✉ 54 E13th Street (and other branches) ☎ 212/475–2018
🚇 N, R, 4, 6 Union Square

### EQUINOX
Everyone's good looking, and a fair bit of eyeing goes on—but what the heck, those bodies took a lot of hard work.

✚ E8 ✉ 897 Broadway (and other branches) ☎ 212/780–9300
🚇 N, R 23rd Street

### JIVAMUKTI YOGA CENTER
Without a doubt, the trendiest ashram in town.

✚ F11 ✉ 6 Astor Place, 404 Lafayette Street ☎ 212/353–0214
🚇 F, S Broadway/Lafayette

### PRINTING HOUSE
A friendly sort of place with classes, a rooftop pool, squash courts and a sundeck.

✚ D12 ✉ 421 Hudson Street ☎ 212/243–7600 🚇 1, 2, 3, 9
Houston Street

### REEBOK SPORTS CLUB NY
Everything from ski and windsurfing simulators to fancy bistro, and huge prices.

✚ b8 ✉ 160 Columbus Avenue
☎ 212/362–6800 🚇 1, 2, 3, 9
66th Street

### VANDERBILT YMCA
Classes, two good pools and no snooty attitude.

✚ G3 ✉ 224 E47th Street
☎ 212/756–9600 🚇 6 51st Street

### WORLD
Half spiritual haven, half professional iron-pumper's heaven—it's light and spacious, and it's open 24 hours.

✚ b8 ✉ 1926 Broadway
☎ 212/874–0942 🚇 1, 2, 3, 9
66th Street

### WHERE DO YOU WORK OUT?

Many of the things people used to do at frenetic all night dance clubs—meet, sweat, schmooze, pose—are now accomplished at the gym. All New Yorkers have gym membership. Most use it. "Where do you work out?" is a perfectly reasonable question, as unsurprising as the sight of people bouncing rhythmically in upstairs windows. Or, more likely, doing their sun salutations, since yoga is the favorite obsession.

*The New York gym provides more than just exercise, it's a way of life*

61

# "Only in New York City"

### BARNEY'S WAREHOUSE SALE

Warehouse sales are known elsewhere, but you must understand, Barney's is *the* store where every single New Yorker bar none aspires to shop for clothes. Consequently, *everyone* goes to this event. It is a zoo.

 D9 ✉ 255 W17th Street 🕐 Feb, Sep
Ⓜ 1 18th Street

### BASKETBALL STARS ON THE STREET

At "The Cage" you can see basketball played by future stars, as good as the pros (and it's free).

 E11 ✉ Sixth Avenue (W3rd Street)
Ⓜ A, B, C, D, E, F W4th Street

### GRAND MARCH OF THE DACHSHUNDS

This is the climax of the two-hour Dachshund Octoberfest (usually the third Saturday at noon). The short-legged dogs parade around the fountain.

 E11 ✉ Washington Square Park
Ⓜ N, R 8th Street

### HOWARD STERN

If he didn't invent the genre of "shock jock," this irritating, self-consciously controversial individual certainly popularized it. To hear him, tune in to FM 92.3 WXRK, Monday to Friday mornings.

*Macy's Thanksgiving Day Parade*

### MACY'S THANKSGIVING DAY PARADE BALLOON INFLATION

Macy's Thanksgiving Day Parade is a real treat, but better are the impromptu street parties that convene the night before, as the balloons go up.

 b6 ✉ Central Park West around 81st Street Ⓜ C 81st Street

### POETRY SLAMS

These are competitive poetry readings. One night a week (Friday is normal at this place) writers declaim, chant, even sing their work to raucous crowds.

 J11 ✉ Nuyorican Poets Café, 236 E3rd Street (Avenues B/C)
☎ 212/505–8183 Ⓜ F Second Avenue

### WIGSTOCK

This fab Labor Day fest is as it sounds—an excuse to wear wild wigs, wild drag and dish. RuPaul started here. Launched in 1984 by the very glam Lady Bunny, it now attracts up to 50,000 *faaabulous* revelers to Pier 54 in the West Village.

### RUSSIAN BATHS

This has been here forever and looks that way in the Stone Room, hot as hell, where you get your *schwitze*—a beating with soapy oak leaves.

 H10 ✉ 268 E10th Street ☎ 212/473–8806 Ⓜ 6 Astor Place

# NEW YORK CITY
## where to...

# Classic

**BRUNCH**

It's hard to imagine what New Yorkers did before the invention of brunch. These days the weekend noontime meal can be everything from the basic omelette to a multi-course culinary adventure. The following are some perennial favorites. Go early or late to avoid the crowds

**Sarabeth's**
✉ Hotel Wales, 1295 Madison Avenue
☎ 212/410–7335

**Bubby's**
✉ 120 Hudson Street
☎ 212/219–0666

**Petite Abeille**
✉ 466 Hudson Street
☎ 212/741–6479

**Time Cafe**
✉ 2330 Broadway
☎ 212/579–5100

**Tea & Sympathy**
✉ 108 Greenwich Avenue
☎ 212/807–8329

**LE BERNADIN ($$$)**
Frenchman Eric Ripert is generally acknowledged to be the fish maestro. Although his deep-carpeted palace of a dress-up restaurant offers non-piscine options, you'd be silly to fork out for one of the city's top tables—and biggest checks—if you weren't a seafood fan. Exquisite, inventive dishes are served by waiters who practically polish your shoes, they are so attentive. Prix fixe only.
⊞ D2 ✉ 155 W51st Street (Sixth/Seventh avenues) ☎ 212/489–7464 🚇 B, D, F, Q 47th–50th streets, Rockefeller Center

**CHANTERELLE ($$$)**
Serene restaurant on a quiet TriBeCa corner. Billowy curtains, flower arrangements and elegant tables provide the perfect backdrop for a romantic evening. The seafood sausage is a dream.
⊞ E14 ✉ 2 Harrison Street (Hudson Street) ☎ 212/966–6960 🕔 Closed Sun, Mon lunch 🚇 1, 9 Franklin Street

**LE CIRQUE 2000 ($$$)**
A veritable circus of the stars; Le Cirque 2000 is the city's pre-eminent spot to see and be seen. The decor defies description—think Versailles meets Disney—and the food strives for greatness.
⊞ F2 ✉ New York Palace Hotel, 455 Madison Avenue (51st Street) ☎ 212/794–9292 🕔 Closed Sun 🚇 6 51st Street

**DANIEL ($$$)**
Perhaps the most formal restaurant in the city, with its salmon-pink walls and columned arches. Serves exquisitely restrained, modern French dishes—opt for the *degustation* menu to fully appreciate chef Daniel Boulud's brilliance. Dessert arrives with its own "basket" of warm madeleines.
⊞ e9 ✉ 60 E65th Street (Madison/Park avenues) ☎ 212/288–0033 🕔 Closed Sun 🚇 6 68th Street

**GRAMERCY TAVERN ($$–$$$)**
As food temples go, Gramercy is quite laid-back, especially if you eat in the less expensive no-reservations tavern area in front, where the food is more rustic, but the same incredible wine list is available. Tom Colicchio uses only the freshest market produce in his hearty, utterly reliable new-American food. He's giving himself competition at Craft, through (► 65).
⊞ F8 ✉ 42 E20th Street (Broadway/Park Avenue) ☎ 212/477–0777 🚇 6, N, R 23rd Street

**JEAN-GEORGES ($$$)**
One of the world's—let alone New York's—great chefs, Alsace native Jean Georges Vongerichten's refined, full-flavored Asian-accented style cannot be imitated. The spacious glass-walled minimalist rooms feel serene and special—perhaps because they were Feng-Shui-ed? Don't miss the molten-center chocolate cake.
⊞ b9 ✉ Central Park West ☎ 212/299–3900 🚇 A, C, 1, 9, B, C Columbus Circle

# Contemporary

### AKA CAFÉ ($)

An ex-Jean Georges chef's small Lower East Side foodie revolution spawned this adorable, relaxed café where Latin-American "small plates" are the price of a deli sandwich, but far more interesting. Try the various empanadas or the hangar steak on a bialy.

✚ J12 ✉ 49 Clinton Street ☎ 212/979–6096 🕐 Closed lunch 🚇 F Second Avenue

### AUREOLE ($$$)

Stunning American cuisine followed by desserts that end every meal with a bang. Conservatively fashionable dining room, with magnificent flower arrangements. Eating in the tiny garden is a treat.

✚ F1 ✉ 34 E61st Street ☎ 212/319–1660 🕐 Closed Sat, Sun lunch 🚇 4 ,5, 6 59th Street

### CRAFT ($$)

Gramercy's Tom Colicchio started a whole new trend here, where fish, deceptively simple and plain, dishes are mixed up by you, the diner, into interesting combos. Great for control freaks, picky eaters and wannabe chefs; not for the lazy.

✚ F8 ✉ 43 E19th Street ☎ 212/780–0880 🕐 Closed Sat lunch, Mon dinner 🚇 N, Q, R, W, 4, 5, 6 Union Square

### FIAMMA ($$)

Three sleek stories connected via a glass elevator. An intimate, small-crowd-pleaser, showcaasing chef Michael White's fresh modern Italian food. Diners depart

with a tiny box of truffles.

✚ E13 ✉ 206 Spring Street ☎ 212/653–0100 🚇 C, E, Spring Street

### GOTHAM BAR AND GRILL ($$$)

This restaurant lives up to its name—befitting an urban megalopolis—and epitomizes New York grandeur. World-class dishes like rack of lamb with swiss chard and roasted shallots have delighted New Yorkers since 1984. The soaring space is light and airy with huge, modern chandeliers and classical accents.

✚ E10 ✉ 12 E12th Street ☎ 212/620–4020 🕐 Closed Sat, Sun lunch 🚇 N, R, 4, 6 Union Square

### MERCER KITCHEN ($$$)

An underground oasis of exposed brick, sleek lines, dim lighting and elegant accents—such as the orchid on each table. The scene is electric and the food lives up to the hype, with exquisitely casual offerings like wood grilled shrimp with garlic confit.

✚ F12 ✉ Mercer Hotel, 147 Mercer Street ☎ 212/966–5454 🚇 N, R Prince Street

### UNION PACIFIC ($$$)

From the wall of falling water at the entrance to the banquettes and caring service, a meal here is an event. Chef Rocco DiSpirito, Italian of descent, is conversant in every culinary tradition, from Thai to French. An unusual variety of wines by the glass tops it off.

✚ F8 ✉ 111 E22nd Street ☎ 212/995–8500 🕐 Closed Sun 🚇 6 23rd Street

### DOING LUNCH

For Restaurant Week, each June, many of the better restaurants in the city offer a prix-fixe lunch in which the price corresponds to the year ($20.00 in the year 2000). Some of the restaurants continue the deal through Labor Day, and it is the best way to dine at serious restaurants for discount prices. Some of the annual favorites include:

Felidia (▶ 69), Gotham Bar and Grill (▶ 65), Nobu (▶ 68), Le Cirque 2000 (▶ 64), Chanterelle (▶ 64), Aureole (▶ 65), Le Bernadin (▶ 64)

# World Cuisines

## LIQUOR LAWS

The legal drinking age in New York is 21 years. If you think your age could be questioned, come prepared with a legal photo ID (such as a passport) for entry into bars and clubs. Liquor stores are closed on Sundays, although beer can be purchased at supermarkets and delis.

### CHEZ ES SAADA ($$)

Fantasy Morocco engulfs you as you descend the rose-petal-strewn stairs to a basement dining room full of Moorish carvings and velvety brocaded nooks and crannies. No culinary revelations here; this is a fun night out—with delightful cocktails.
➕ G12 ✉ 42 E1st Street (First/Second avenues) ☎ 212/777–5617 🕓 Closed lunch 🚇 F Second Avenue

### EIGHT MILE CREEK ($$)

Australian cuisine? What's that, you ask? This tiny Nolita gem may be the only place in this hemisphere to answer that confidently. Ostrich carpaccio or seared kangaroo may sound pretentious, but this food is yummy and as friendly as its continent. Below is a big, noisy and popular bar.
➕ G12 ✉ 240 Mulberry Street (Prince/Spring streets) ☎ 212/431–4635 🕓 Closed lunch 🚇 6 Spring Street; F, S Broadway Lafayette

### PATRIA ($$$)

"Nuevo Latino" cuisine provides astonishing combinations, bright flavors and plenty of spice. The fried snapper and Patria pork entrées on the prix-fixe only menu pay homage to their Latin roots while becoming something completely new—much like Patria.
➕ F8 ✉ 250 Park Avenue South (20th Street) ☎ 212/777–6211 🕓 Closed Sun 🚇 N, R 23rd Street

### PERIYALI ($$)

Waiters at this pretty place are so sweet, dinner feels like a Greek Island vacation. A big menu includes the usual *stifado*, *moussaka*, *kleftides* and so on, but there are many unusual dishes you'd be hard-pressed to find in Athens. Try for a table in the gorgeous greenhouse.
➕ E8 ✉ 35 W20th Street (Fifth/Sixth avenues) 🕓 Closed Sun 🚇 6, N, R 23rd Street

### PONGAL ($)

Come here to enjoy the fragrant vegetarian cooking of the southern regions of India. If the menu intimidates, order one of the *thalis* so you can sample several dishes. By the way, it's strictly kosher.
➕ F7 ✉ 110 Lexington Avenue (27th/28th streets) ☎ 212/696–9458 🚇 6 23th Street

### ROSA MEXICANO ($$$)

This perennial favorite is always a fiesta—loud, colorful and crowded. The menu consists of upscale versions of authentic Mexican dishes and there isn't a loser on the list. Three different rooms offer diners various moods.
➕ H1 ✉ 1063 First Avenue (58th Street) ☎ 212/753–7407 🚇 4, 5, 6 59th Street

### TABLA ($$$)

A grand staircase leads to a pink and green dining room at its best by night. This was the city's first foray into Indian–fusion, and it can yield astonishing new flavors.
➕ F7 ✉ 11 Madison Avenue (25th Street) ☎ 212/889–0667 🕓 Closed Sun lunch 🚇 6 23rd Street

# Diners, Delis & Pizza

**ARTURO'S PIZZERIA ($)**
Don't go for the decor, or the service, and definitely don't go for quiet conversation. Go for some of the best coal-oven pizza in town, in a lively, sometimes raucous, setting. The dough is slightly thicker than the classic Neapolitan variety but the crusty pie will satisfy a any pizza-lover's craving.
➕ E12 ✉ 106 Houston Street (Thompson Street) ☎ 212/677–3820 🕐 Closed lunch 🚇 1, 9 Houston Street

**BARNEY GREENGRASS ($$)**
BG serves classic Jewish breakfast fare like bagels, cream cheese and the definitive smoked sturgeon. An individual *babka* (chocolate streusel danish) will take the edge off while you wait upward of an hour for your table.
➕ a5 ✉ 541 Amsterdam Avenue (86th Street) ☎ 212/724–4707 🕐 Closed Mon 🚇 1, 9 86th Street

**CAFE HABANA ($)**
A modern lunch counter with Latin diner fare like Cuban sandwiches and unmissable grilled Mexican corn. Very popular with the hip, downtown crowd.
➕ G12 ✉ 17 Prince Street (Elizabeth Street) ☎ 212/625–2001 🚇 6 Spring Street

**CARNEGIE DELI ($$)**
Mile-high sandwiches are the draw at this New York institution—one is enough to feed a small army (but beware the sharing charge). A favorite of

theater types and deli lovers, it's a cliché, but also a place you've got to try to really experience the city.
➕ D2 ✉ 854 Seventh Avenue (55th Street) ☎ 212/757–2245 🚇 N, R Seventh Avenue

**KIEV ($)**
This quintessential Eastern European diner, complete with abrupt Slavic waitresses, serves hearty food around the clock. The potato pancakes are ample and greasy, perfect with a dish of applesauce.
➕ G10 ✉ 117 Second Avenue (7th Street) ☎ 212/674–4040 🕐 Open 24 hours 🚇 6 Astor Place

**LOMBARDI'S ($)**
The aroma of thin crust pies emerging from the coal oven, red checked tablecloths, scarred tables and seasoned waitresses set the mood for some of the best pizza in Manhattan.
➕ G13 ✉ 32 Spring Street (Mott/Mulberry streets) ☎ 212/941–7994 🚇 6 Spring Street

**SECOND AVENUE DELI ($–$$)**
One of the last of the real New York delis—New Yorkers who remember the good-old-days will travel across the city to feed their food cravings. A recent renovation may have removed some of the patina, but don't be fooled, it sure is the real thing.
➕ G10 ✉ 156 Second Avenue (10th Street) ☎ 212/677–0606 🚇 6 Astor Place

**LATE-NIGHT MUNCHIES**

There are restaurants in New York where you may have to wait for a table, even at 3am. Late-night restaurants range from raffish dives, to chic eateries, to dark lounges, to ethnic excursions. These are some of the most popular after-hours haunts (for good reason).
**Florent** (24 hours)
✉ 69 Gansvoort Street
☎ 212/989–5779
**First** (till 2am)
✉ 87 First Avenue
☎ 212/674–3823
**Kang Suh** (24 hours)
✉ 1250 Broadway
☎ 212/564–6845
**Corner Bistro** (till 4am)
✉ 331 W4th Street
☎ 212/242–9502
**Lansky Lounge** (till 4am)
✉ 138 Delancey
☎ 212/677–9489
**Big Nick's Pizza and Burger Joint** (closed from 5–6am)
✉ 2175 Broadway
☎ 212/362–9238

# Asian

### GIANT SUSHI

For the sushi connoisseur, Yama (\$–\$\$) may not offer the best there is, but it does serve the biggest sushi and it is very good. Sadly, many people share this view, and the tiny place is engulfed with salivating sushi wolves, lining up for hours.

➕ F9 ✉ 49 Irving Place (17th Street) ☎ 212/475-0969 🕐 Closed Sun 🚇 N, R, 4, 5, 6 14th Street (Union Square)

### BLUE RIBBON SUSHI (\$\$\$)

Terrific freshness and exotic offerings all go to keep this wood-paneled sushi bar abuzz; a good sake selection, served in the traditional wooden boxes.

➕ E13 ✉ 119 Sullivan Street (Prince/Spring streets) ☎ 212/343-0404 🕐 Closed lunch, Mon 🚇 C, E Spring Street

### GREAT NY NOODLE TOWN (\$)

A no-frills Chinatown restaurant with superb Cantonese food. Specialties include crispy baby pig, salt-baked softshell crab and, as the name implies, anything with noodles.

➕ G14 ✉ 28 Bowery (Bayard Street) ☎ 212/349-0923 🚇 F, E Broadway

### JING FONG (\$)

No foray into Chinatown is complete without the dim sum experience, and Jing Fung is where it's most overwhelming. Trolleys laden with everything from steamed pork buns to stewed chicken feet whizz through a room the size of a football stadium—it's up to you to hail them before the best bits are gone. Go with a veteran if you can; the servers are too harried to help.

➕ G14 ✉ 20 Elizabeth Street (Bayard/Canal streets) ☎ 212/964-5256 🕐 Go before 3pm 🚇 6, N, R Canal Street

### KOM TANG SOOT BUL HOUSE (\$–\$\$)

In the middle of a block full of Korean restaurants, this bi-level emporium offers a great taste of the cuisine. Go for the messy, delicious fun of a tabletop barbecue.

➕ E6 ✉ 32 W32nd Street (Fifth Avenue) ☎ 212/947-8482 🚇 B, D, N, F, R 34th Street

### NOBU (\$\$\$)

It is difficult to get a reservation at this TriBeCa Japanese shrine but patience and persistence is rewarded by the hauntingly delicious cooking. The dining room is modern Japanese fantasy with lots of bamboo.

➕ E14 ✉ 105 Hudson Street (Franklin Street) ☎ 212/219-0500 🕐 Closed Sat, Sun lunch 🚇 1, 9 Franklin Street

### REPUBLIC (\$)

A noisy, inexpensive and useful restaurant on Union Square where trendy people slurp noodles while sitting at communal tables in a re-creation of an Asian cafeteria. A super choice for a quick bite—the service is miraculously fast—or an evening of people-watching.

➕ F9 ✉ 37 Union Square West (16th/17th streets) ☎ 212/627-7172 🚇 4, 5, 6, N, R, L Union Square

### VIET-NAM (\$)

Don't be put off by the dingy surroundings, this basement dive serves some of the best, least expensive Vietnamese food in New York, with lots of choices.

➕ G14 ✉ 11–13 Doyers Street (Bowery/Pell streets) ☎ 212/693-0725 🚇 6 Canal Street

# Italian & Mediterranean

## BABBO ($$$)
On a quiet street off Washington Square Park, this elegant duplex has the feel of a Roman *ristorante*—untamed flower arrangements and an informal bar area. This is Mario Batali's showcase for his unbelievable pan-Italian cooking. Nobody else comes close. Reserve well in advance.
🕀 E11 ✉ 110 Waverly Place (McDougal Street/Sixth Avenue) ☎ 212/777–0303 🕘 Closed lunch 🚇 A, C, E, B, D, F W4th Street

## BAR PITTI ($)
In summer this loveable no-frills, marble-floored Tuscan trattoria comes into its own with rows of sidewalk tables, but it's a great hideaway in the colder months too. Expect a wait—it's an open secret that the pastas, grills and marinated vegetables are great value.
🕀 E12 ✉ 268 Sixth Avenue (Bleecker/Houston streets) ☎ 212/982–3300 🚇 A, B, C, D, E, F, Q W4th Street

## IL BUCO ($$–$$$)
There's a dinner-party feel at this unabashedly cluttered restaurant bursting with treasures from yesteryear. Great Mediterranean food, such as orata baked in sea salt, or *stinco di vitello tartufato*.
🕀 G11 ✉ 47 Bond Street (Bowery/Lafayette streets) ☎ 212/533–1932 🕘 Closed Sun, Mon lunch 🚇 6, B, F Bleecker Street

## COL LEGNO ($)
This East Village Tuscan restaurant has it all, from an appealing, simple menu of pastas (try the wild boar *pappardelle*), pizzas and grills—from the wood-burning oven in the corner—to no-fuss service and decent prices.
🕀 G10 ✉ 231 E9th Street (Second/Third avenues) ☎ 212/777–4650 🚇 6 Astor Place

## FELIDIA ($$$)
Midtown formal Italian restaurant with an emphasis on Friulian classics. Game, pasta and risotto dishes are expertly prepared. The impressive wine list is heavy on rare Italian selections.
🕀 G1 ✉ 243 E58th Street (Second Avenue) ☎ 212/758–1479 🕘 Closed Sat, Sun lunch 🚇 6 59th Street

## PROVENCE ($$)
A longtime favorite on SoHo's western edge, this romantic bistro is provençal by name and by nature, with a flower-bedecked interior, friendly service, southern French cooking and, to top it all, one of the sweetest gardens in town.
🕀 E12 ✉ 38 MacDougal Street (Prince Street) ☎ 212/475–7500 🚇 C, E Spring Street

## I TRULLI ($$$)
One of New York's most authentic Italian experiences. The wood-burning oven is kept busy, and all the pastas and ricotta are made in house. A casual wine bar is adjacent to the main dining room and there is a beautiful garden.
🕀 F7 ✉ 122 E27th Street (Lexington Avenue) ☎ 212/481–7372 🕘 Closed Sat lunch, Sun 🚇 6 28th Street

## ON THE GO
A slice, of pizza that is, is probably the favorite "fast food" of New Yorkers, and indeed most neighborhood pizzerias proffer pies that will satisfy. But New York has recently spawned a plethora of "gourmet" fast-food stores that will provide well prepared, tasty choices for those without the time for a "real" meal.

**Bread**
✉ 20 Spring Street
☎ 212/334–1015

**Better Burger**
✉ 565 Third Avenue
☎ 212/949–7528

**Cosi Sandwich Bar**
✉ 60 E56th Street
☎ 212/588–0888;
✉ 38 E45th Street
☎ 212/949–7400

**Daily Soup**
✉ 2 Rector Street
☎ 212/945–7687

**F&B**
✉ 269 W23rd Street
☎ 646/486–4441

**Hampton Chutney Co.**
✉ 68 Prince Street
☎ 212/226–9996

**Mangia**
✉ 16 E48th Street
☎ 212/754–7600;
✉ 50 W57th Street
☎ 212/582–5554

# Comfort Food

## TERMINAL FEEDING

The best thing about the Grand Central renovations is the Food Court on the lower level. The idea was to install outposts of New York's favorite casual eateries to re-create the melting pot in miniature—and it worked. Some highlights:

**Café Spice** (☎ 212/227–1300) is an undemanding pleasant place from the Central Village, with curries a step up from 6th Street.

**Caviarteria** (☎ 212/682–5355) is as it sounds—fish eggs and champagne for commuters; quite lunatic.

**Custard Beach** (☎ 212/983–9155) is all about the richest, bestest vanilla ice cream (ignore the other flavors).

**Junior's** (☎ 212/983–5257) is a great diner and a Brooklyn institution, most famous for its peerless super-rich cheesecake.

**Knödel** (☎ 212/986–1230) does wurst, *boudin, merguez*—in short, global sausages.

**Mendy's Kosher Delicatessen** (☎ 212/856–9399) does knishes and pastrami-on-rye for those who can't get to Katz's.

## BALTHAZAR ($$–$$$)

A re-created Paris brasserie, complete with red banquettes and wine choices written on the mirrored walls. The delicious food, like the seafood platters from the raw bar, keep the celebrity crowds coming back.
➕ F12 ✉ 80 Spring Street (Broadway/Crosby Street) ☎ 212/965–1414 🚇 6 Spring Street

## BLUE RIBBON ($$–$$$)

This small American bistro is a popular late-night hangout for chefs. In the front window Alonso shells fresh oysters and prepares towering seafood platters. The menu offers everything from a hamburger, to foie gras, to motzoh ball soup.
➕ E12 ✉ 97 Sullivan Street (Prince/Spring streets) ☎ 212/274–0404 🚫 Closed Mon lunch 🚇 C, E Spring Street

## LA BONNE SOUPE ($–$$)

This is that Midtown rarity—a reasonably priced, casual restaurant. Soup is the staple in this anachronistic checkered-tablecloth French bistro, and trendy-again cheese fondue is another specialty.
➕ E2 ✉ 48 W55th Street (Fifth/Sixth avenues) ☎ 212/586–7650 🚇 N, R Fifth Avenue

## CAFÉ LOUP ($)

The name is French and the menu is in French (with translation), but this cozy Village bistro is secretly very Manhattan—the soft-focus Manhattan of Woody Allen's quainter movies, that is. The big

menu features everything you could possibly crave, the service is delightful, the tables are candlelit; everyone loves it here.
➕ D9 ✉ 105 W13th Street (Sixth/Seventh avenues) ☎ 212/255–4746 🚇 1, 2, 3, 9, F 14th Street

## CHAT'N'CHEW ($)

This gaudy, kitsch fifties soda fountain of a place down the block from Union Square appeals to NYU students and kids of all ages, with huge plates of heartland food—catfish po'boys, BLTs, mac and cheese, meatloaf and so on.
➕ E9 ✉ 10 E16th Street (Fifth Avenue/Union Square) ☎ 212/243–1616 🚇 4, 5, 6, L, N, R Union Square 14th Street

## LE JARDIN BISTRO ($)

Bouillabaisse at a garden table under the rampant grapevines on a summer night here is heaven—as is cassoulet or coq au vin in the simple dining room on a winter's day. The Francophile's search for the ideal bistro ends here.
➕ F13 ✉ 25 Cleveland Place (Spring/Kenmare streets) ☎ 212/343–9599 🚇 6, Spring Street

## THE RED CAT ($–$$)

Jimmy Bradley's red-painted, laid-back restaurant is the best bet for dinner after gallery-hopping in West Chelsea. It's all a bit Southern Italy (think sweet pea risotto cake), right down to the sunny atmosphere.
➕ B7 ✉ 227 Tenth Avenue (23rd/24th streets) ☎ 212/242–1122 🚇 C, E 23rd Street

# Classic New York City

## CAFE DES ARTISTES ($$$)

Howard Chandler Christy murals adorn this romantic, art-nouveau dining room, where Old-World style reigns. The menu is an appealing mix of Hungarian and French dishes, from sturgeon schnitzel to *pot au feu*.
✛ b8 ✉ 1 W67th Street (Central Park West/Columbus Avenue) ☎ 212/877–3500 🚇 1, 9 66th Street

## FOUR SEASONS ($$$)

Every once in a while a restaurant defines an age, and then transcends it. The Four Seasons defined the "power lunch" and changed the face of New York dining. The dark wood-paneled Grill Room makes all diners seem like media moguls, but the romantic Pool Room makes anything seem possible. In such a grand setting the food is almost besides the point, but the seasonal menu provides many delicious options.
✛ F2 ✉ 99 E52nd Street (Park/Lexington avenues) ☎ 212/754–9494 🕐 Closed Sat lunch, Sun 🚇 6 51st Street

## OYSTER BAR ($–$$)

Whether at the long counter or in the wood-paneled dining room, some bivalves or molluscs, clam chowder or grilled fish in the 1913 vaulted Guastavino-tiled rooms in Grand Central is a thoroughly New York experience.
✛ F4 ✉ Grand Central, lower level, Vanderbilt Avenue (42nd Street) ☎ 212/490–6650 🚇 4, 5, 6, 7 Grand Central 42nd Street

## PETER LUGER ($$$)

You get steak, some hash browns and creamed spinach for the table, and maybe some tomato-and-onion salad to start—that's it, and that's all you need. It's not about atmosphere or fine wines, its not about feeling special, it's about steak. Since 1887 this landmark has been serving the best beef in New York.
✛ Off map ✉ 178 Broadway (Bedford Avenue), Brooklyn ☎ 718/387–7400 🚇 J, M, Z Marcy Avenue

## '21' CLUB ($$$)

This restaurant has been famous from its speakeasy days—so much so that it has a "21" merchandise store. In the main room, dine beneath a ceiling strung with thousands of toy trucks. "Upstairs at 21" is the new, even pricier, upper floor salon.
✛ E2 ✉ 21 W52nd Street (Fifth/Sixth avenues) ☎ 212/582–7200 🕐 Closed Sun 🚇 B, D, F 47th–50th streets

## UNION SQUARE CAFÉ ($$–$$$)

Genius restaurateur Danny Meyer's original place is now old enough to qualify as a classic. You are guaranteed a good time in the friendliest upscale dining room anywhere. Michael Romano's cooking is indispensable. Choosing is agony—it's all so good, from *porcini risotto* to the fresh tuna burger that was born here. Don't skip dessert; surely you can manage the cookie plate?
✛ E9 ✉ 21 E16th Street (Fifth Avenue/Union Square) ☎ 212/243–4020 🚇 6, L, N, R 14th Street Union Square

## WHAT SHALL WE EAT TONIGHT?

When you live in New York, responses to this dilemma include: Mexican, Southwestern, Cajun, Southern, Italian, French, Spanish, Japanese, Chinese, Vietnamese, Caribbean, Brazilian, Cuban, Chino-Latino, Jewish, Polish, Hungarian, Ukrainian, Greek, Irish, British, Austrian, Swedish, Thai, Korean, Indonesian, Malaysian, Indian, Peruvian, Tibetan, Burmese, Ethiopian, Afghan, Lebanese or Moroccan food. Even American. In New York you soon get familiar with every national and regional cuisine, as well as most permutations of hybrid.

# Neighborhoods & Streets

## BORN TO SHOP

As with everything else, New Yorkers are passionate about shopping. If there is something made somewhere in the world, chances are you can buy it here—and it often sells for less than it does wherever it came from. The city has been overrun recently with so many chain stores that some avenues feel like outdoor malls. But there are still pockets of interesting, independent retailers everywhere. When a handful of stores selling similar items congregate along a street or in a neighborhood, New Yorkers sometimes refer to the area as a "district." There's a flower district (W28th Street between Sixth and Seventh avenues), a discount perfume district (E17th Street between Fifth Avenue and Union Square West), a lighting district (The Bowery south of Spring), a photography district (Flatiron side streets between Fifth and Sixth avenues) and many more. Most of these places are set up for wholesale (trade) sales, but almost all will deal directly with the public (retail).

## AVENUE OF THE AMERICAS

Superstores line the stretch between 18th and 23rd streets (and straggle up to Macy's at 34th Street). Bargain hunt at TJ Maxx, Filene's Basement and Bed Bath and Beyond. Goodman's Treasures has an eclectic collection of home furnishings and there's a big branch of Barnes & Noble for books. E8 F 23rd Street, Path Train

## CANAL STREET

The main drag of Chinatown between West Broadway and Mott Street is an irresistibly gaudy source of bogus brands: faux Gucci, Chanel, Hermès, you name it. Also gold jewelry and discounted electronics. Don't miss Pearl Paint (real art supplies and stationery) and the Pearl River Mart. F14 N, R Canal Street

## ELIZABETH STREET

Center of the chic new Nolita neighborhood, the strip between Spring and Houston streets is lined with tiny stores and restaurants—glass blowers, independent designers and artisanal purveyors on the cutting edge of style. G12 6 Spring Street

## 57TH STREET

Touristy stores and theme restaurants interspersed with high fashion boutiques. Check out Chanel, Prada, Coach and Laura Ashley, then stop for a drink at the Four Seasons Hotel. E1 N, R 57th Street

## LOWER FIFTH AVENUE

Between 14th and 23rd streets, Fifth Avenue has become something of a mall. Gap, Banana Republic and similar stores will dress you in style, for bargains try Daffy's and for cutting-edge women's fashions stop at Intermix. The stores lining the side streets are generally more interesting. E8 N, R 23rd Street, 4, 5, 6, L Union Square

## MADISON AVENUE

It doesn't get any tonier (or more expensive) than this. For clothes Versace, Armani, Valentino, or for shoes Stephane Kélian. Other notables—Crate & Barrel, Donna Karan, Barneys—help to make this a shopper's haven. F2 N, R Fifth Avenue

## SOHO

First it was factories, then galleries, then stores—still some of the trendiest shopping anywhere. Clothing—from Old Navy to Chanel—housewares, jewelry and more in loftlike stores. Check out Rem Koolhaas's Prada store. E12 N, R Prince Street

## UPPER FIFTH AVENUE

Worlds apart from Lower Fifth, the strip between Rockefeller Center and Central Park is home to some of the swankiest stores in town—Sak's, Bendel's, Tiffany's and Bergdorf's to name a few. Top-of-the-line jewelers include Harry Winston and Van Cleef & Arpel's. E2 6 59th Street

# Department Stores

## ABC CARPET AND HOME

Organized like stores at the turn of the 19th century (without any real "departments") the fun at this giant home furnishings emporium is to wander the floors to sift through the treasures. Everything is for sale, even the tables and chairs in the Parlor Café. The new food store (attached to the café) is a welcome addition.

➕ F8 ✉ 888 Broadway (19th Street) ☎ 212/473–3000 🚇 4, 5, 6, L, N, R Union Square

## BARNEYS

The epicenter of affluent, fashion-forward New Yorkers has a challenger in the Meatpacking District's Jeffrey, but it's holding its own. Designers from around the world are represented. Makeup, housewares, food and accessories are all among the finest.

➕ F1 ✉ 660 Madison Avenue (61st Street) ☎ 212/826–8900 🚇 4, 6 59th Street

## BERGDORF GOODMAN

A more exclusive department store would be difficult to imagine. Women's clothing, makeup, extraordinary housewares and a café are on the West side of Fifth Avenue, while menswear and haberdashery are across the street. Don't be intimidated, walk in like you own the place and the service will be superb.

➕ E1 ✉ 754, 745 Fifth Avenue (57th Street) ☎ 212/753–7300 🚇 4, 6 59th Street

## BLOOMINGDALE'S

When the affluent residents of the Upper East Side need to pick something up, they look here first. In addition to clothing, furniture, linens and housewares are all top notch.

➕ G1 ✉ 1000 Third Avenue (59th Street) ☎ 212/705–2000 🚇 4, 6 59th Street

## MACY'S

The sign outside says it's the largest store in the world, and by the time you've made your way across the nine block-long floors of this grandfather of all department stores, you'll believe them. Everything (including thousands of other shoppers) is here.

➕ D5 ✉ 151 W34th Street (Herald Square) ☎ 212/695–4400 🚇 B, D, F, N, R 34th Street

## SAK'S FIFTH AVENUE

The original of what is now a nationwide brand retains some vestige of the elegant air of Old New York, especially in the wood-paneled street level and the women's boutiques.

➕ E3 ✉ 611 Fifth Avenue (50th Street) ☎ 212/753–4000 🚇 E, F Fifth Avenue

## TAKASHIMAYA

An austere Japanese esthetic informs the atmosphere of this small but exquisite department store. Housewares and gifts are the main focus, but you'll stumble across other finds as well.

➕ E2 ✉ 693 Fifth Avenue (55th Street) ☎ 212/350–0115 🚇 E, F Fifth Avenue

## PEARL RIVER MART

You can't see this Chinese department store from the street, though it's got three floors filled with stuff and two entrances. Shop here, in an atmosphere reminiscent of some household consumer shrine of the 1950s, for chrome lunch pails with clip-on lids; embroidered silk pajamas and Suzy Wong dresses; bamboo fans and porcelain rice bowls—all the things, in fact, you can get in the smaller Chinatown emporia, but collected under one roof. The food department sells both dried squid and English cookies. The prices are very, very low.

➕ F14 ✉ 277 Canal Street (Broadway) ☎ 212/431–4770 🚇 N, R Canal Street

# Clothes

**MORE SHOPS**

**Agnès B**
✉ 1063 Madison Avenue
☎ 212/570–9333
**Armani Exchange**
✉ 568 Broadway
☎ 212/431–6000
**Chanel**
✉ 5 E57th Street
☎ 212/355–5050
**Comme des Garçons**
✉ 520 W22nd Street
☎ 212/604–9200
**Daryl K**
✉ 42 Bond Street
☎ 212/777–0713
**Gianni Versace**
✉ 817 Madison Avenue
☎ 212/744–6868
**Gucci**
✉ 685 Fifth Avenue
☎ 212/826–2600
**Intermix Inc**
✉ 27 W20th Street
☎ 212/741–5075
**Marc Jacobs**
✉ 403 Bleecker Street
☎ 212/924–0026
**Polo/Ralph Lauren**
✉ 867 Madison Avenue
(72nd Street)
☎ 212/606–2100
**Yohji Yamamoto**
✉ 103 Grand Street
☎ 212/966–9066

## WOMEN'S

**BETSY JOHNSON**
This long-lived fashion darling produces fun, often outrageous, looks.
✚ b8 ✉ 248 Columbus Avenue (71st Street)
☎ 212/362–3364 🚇 1, 2, 3 72nd Street

**CYNTHIA ROWLEY**
Adorable, hip dresses and shoes. Shop here for a night out on the town.
✚ E12 ✉ 112 Wooster Street
☎ 212/334–1144 🚇 N, R Prince Street

**MORGANE LE FAY**
Liliana Ordas's floaty, yet tailored, slightly theatrical designs. (Branch in SoHo.)
✚ d7 ✉ 746 Madison Avenue (74th Street) ☎ 212/879–9700 🚇 6 77th Street

**NICOLE MILLER**
Girl-about-town Miller designs fun fitted suits, dresses and accessories with tongue in cheek.
✚ d8 ✉ 780 Madison Avenue (66th Street) ☎ 212/288–9779 🚇 6 77th Street

**SCOOP**
Hip labels from Daryl K to Tocca and Katayone Adeli, plus cult items like Petit Bateau T's.
✚ F13 ✉ 532 Broadway (Spring Street) ☎ 212/925–2886 🚇 F, S Broadway Lafayette; N, R Prince Street

## MEN'S

**PAUL SMITH**
Magnificent and expensive menswear for the fashion conscious gentleman.
✚ E9 ✉ 108 Fifth Avenue (16th Street) 🚇 4, 5, 6, N, R, L Union Street

**SEAN**
One-stop shopping for the under-40 set, with cool suits, shirts, sweaters and T-shirts. It's not about the label (many unknown Italians live here), it's the fit, the cut and the service that count.
✚ E12; b9 ✉ 132 Thompson Street (Houston Street); 224 Columbus Avenue (Broadway)
☎ 212/598–5980; 212/769–1489 🚇 F, S Broadway Lafayette; 1, 9, 66th Street Lincoln Center

## BOTH

**A.P.C.**
Simple, ultra-chic clothes, made with durable fabrics.
✚ F12 ✉ 131 Mercer Street
☎ 212/966–9685 🚇 N, R Prince Street

**BROOKS BROTHERS**
The store that practically created the preppy look. But can't be beat for traditional suits, shirts, casual clothes and shoes. Also has a women's line.
✚ F4 ✉ 346 Madison Avenue (45th Street) ☎ 212/682–8800 🚇 4, 6 Grand Central

**PRADA**
More of an art museum than a shop, this temple to Miuccia's perfect taste is a must-see.
✚ F13 ✉ 575 Broadway
☎ 212/334–8888 🚇 N, R Prince Street

**TOOTSI PLOHOUND**
The cutting edge in footwear. Big names, European lines and TP's own label, though none at bargain rates.
✚ E8 ✉ 137 Fifth Avenue (22nd Street) ☎ 212/460–8650 🚇 N, R 23rd Street

# Discount Shopping

## BIG STORES

### CENTURY 21
Practically a cult, especially in the European designer area. Sharpen your elbows.
➕ F17 ✉ 22 Cortlandt Street ☎ 212/227–9092 🚇 N, R City Hall

### DAFFY'S
With some patience, and a lot of sifting through cheap imitations, you can discover some ridiculously inexpensive items for men and women.
➕ E8 ✉ 111 Fifth Avenue ☎ 212/529–4477 🚇 L, N, R, 4, 6 Union Square

### LOEHMANN'S
The Manhattan branch of a Brooklyn institution, this five-floor off-price fashion emporium is best for its Back Room, where the designers—Donna Karan, Calvin Klein, Alberta Feretti, even Valentino—lurk, at small prices.
➕ D8 ✉ 101 Seventh Avenue (17th Street) ☎ 212/352–0856 🚇 1, 9 18th Street

## SMALLER STORES

### FIND OUTLET
Missed all those sample sales? Catch up here—recent season's overflow at great prices.
➕ D9 ✉ 361 W17th Street ☎ 212/243–3177 🚇 1, 9, 19th Street

### KLEIN'S OF MONTICELLO
Orchard Street is known for bargains, but this is the best of the bunch.
➕ H13 ✉ 105 Orchard Street ☎ 212/966–1453 🚇 F Delancey Street

## USED CLOTHES

### ENCORE
Society-lady cast-offs at a fraction of the original price (which can still be hundreds of dollars). We're talking big-name designers, the kind of stuff you would wear to the Oscars. There are a few men's things for sale as well.
➕ d7 ✉ 1132 Madison Avenue ☎ 212/879–2850 🚇 6 77th Street

### INA
Showroom samples and barely worn designer duds. The prices are high, but fair, and there's a men's version round the corner.
➕ E12 ✉ 21 Prince Street ☎ 212/334–9048 🚇 N, R Prince Street

### MICHAEL'S RESALE
Being in the middle of spiffy Madison Avenue, you'd expect quality here, and you get it—Upper East Side ladies don't buy anything without knowing its pedigree. Labels are along the Ferragamo, Ungaro, Valentino axis.
➕ d7 ✉ 2nd Floor, 1041 Madison Avenue ☎ 212/737–7273 🚇 6 77th Street

### BROOKLYN'S DOMSEY WAREHOUSE
Bewildering acres of work clothes, military wear, jeans, prom dresses, vintage stuff sorted by era, plus a department where you pay by the pound.
➕ Off map ✉ 431 Kent Avenue/496 Wythe Avenue ☎ 718/384–6000 🚇 J Marcy Avenue

### SAMPLE SALES
Many top designers—Donna Karan, French Connection, Tocca, Chaiken and Capone, Cynthia Rowley—have yearly sample sales where last season's merchandize is drastically discounted. Held in huge showrooms, the amenities are severely limited and the crowds can often be daunting, but for the fashion and budget conscious they are a must. The best way to find out are through printed advertisements in magazines like *New York Magazine*, or online at www.sample.com. You may even be handed a flyer by someone on the street.

# Superstores

## BIGGER, BETTER

"New Yorkers don't need another boutique," the owner of the nationwide housewares store, Crate & Barrel, declared just before his 54,000-sq ft (5022sq m) showroom opened on Madison Avenue in 1995. Regardless of whether New Yorkers agree with him, since the invasion of the superstores, it's become harder and harder for small, independent boutiques to compete. Will the big fish eat the tadpoles for lunch? It's hard to say. But why shouldn't Manhattanites enjoy up to 45 percent discounts the rest of the country gets from superstore shopping? After all, the city's been through it all before, with no harm done. The last age of the giant department store—including S. Klein's, Wanamaker's, McCreery's, Bonwit Teller and Stern Brothers of Ladies' Mile (Avenue of the Americas)— happened during the closing years of the 19th century.

## BARNES AND NOBLE

In this age of illiteracy, who would have predicted book shopping would become chic? The first B&N superstore opened in 1993—complete with café, tables, easy chairs and a full calendar of events—and quickly acquired a reputation as a singles cruising scene. The Sixth Avenue branch followed, then Astor Place and Union Square. B&N has been a New York institution since 1873. Now for many it's replaced the library.
🕂 a6 ✉ 2289 Broadway (82nd Street) ☎ 212/362–8835, and branches 🚇 1, 9 79th Street

## BED, BATH & BEYOND

The first to reclaim the giant retail spaces of Sixth Avenue, this behemoth is filled with everything for the home. Oddly, the impressive stock doesn't afford much variety, but the prices are good.
🕂 D8 ✉ 620 Sixth Avenue (19th Street) ☎ 212/255–3550 🚇 F 23rd Street

## COMP USA

Like a supermarket for hardware and software, this outpost of a national chain undercuts most of the competition.
🕂 E5 ✉ 420 Fifth Avenue (37th Street) ☎ 212/764–6224 🚇 B, D, F, N, R 34th Street

## CRATE & BARREL

Having refreshed your wardrobe come here for the wardrobe itself, perhaps in cherrywood with cast-iron fixtures? Fashionable housewares and furniture at reasonable prices made New Yorkers adopt this national chain as their own.
🕂 F1 ✉ Madison Avenue (59th Street) ☎ 212/308–0011 🚇 N, R Fifth Avenue

## NIKE TOWN NY

Enter the Spaceship Sneaker and feel like a professional athlete. High-tech videos, multilevel displays and an industrial atmosphere that encourages aerobic shopping makes this a favorite for dads and kids.
🕂 D1 ✉ 11 Pennsylvania Plaza (57th Street) ☎ 212/946–2710 🚇 N, R 57th Street

## STAPLES

The 15 branches of this office-supply superstore have all but forced smaller stationery stores out of business—the best prices by far. The Avenue of the Americas and Union Square stores have the largest selection.
🕂 F9 ✉ 5 Union Square West (15th Street) ☎ 212/929–6323 🚇 4, 5, 6, N, R, L Union Square; 🕂 E8 ✉ 699 Avenue of the Americas (23rd Street) ☎ 212/675–5698 🚇 F, Path, 23rd Street

## TOWER RECORDS

The three branches of this New York music and entertainment warehouse attract a diverse crowd. The original on lower Broadway (which also has book and video departments) was the first and remains the favorite among die-hard fans.
🕂 F11 ✉ 692 Broadway (4th Street) ☎ 212/505–1500 🚇 F, S Broadway/Lafayette

# Food

## CHELSEA MARKET
A block-long urban gourmet shopping mall with meat, fish, baked goods, produce, restaurant supplies, wines and specialty purveyors.
✚ C9 ✉ 75 Ninth Avenue (15th Street) ☎ 212/243–6005 🚇 A, C, E 14th Street; L Eighth Avenue

## CITARELLA
This fish specialist is a Broadway food shrine.
✚ a7 ✉ 2135 Broadway (75th Street) ☎ 212/874–0383 🚇 1, 9, 2, 3 72nd Street

## DEAN & DELUCA
A loft-like space with white-washed walls, artistic displays and chic foodstuffs from around the world. Every item has its own gallery—piles of cookies; towers of spices in tiny chrome canisters; baskets of onion ficelles; and the best (and most expensive) cheese selection in the city. A coffee bar at the entrance offers good snacks.
✚ F12 ✉ 560 Broadway (Prince Street) ☎ 212/431–8350 🚇 N, R Prince Street

## FAIRWAY
Get a taste of Upper West Side everyday life at this bewilderingly comprehensive grocery.
✚ a7 ✉ 2127 Broadway (75th Street) ☎ 212/595–1888 🚇 1, 9, 2, 3 72nd Street

## GOURMET GARAGE
The place to find yellow cherry tomatoes, dried cherries, fresh clams, truffle butter, smoked duck, gelati, you-name-it, and it only *acts* like it's bargain-priced.
✚ F13 ✉ 435 Broome Street (Mercer Street) ☎ 212/941–5850 🚇 N, R Prince Street

## GREENMARKET
Farmers travel year-round from the tri-state area to this outdoor farmers market that has rejuvenated the entire Union Square area.
✚ F9 🚇 4, 5, 6, N, R, L Union Square

## KALUSTYAN'S
If it's ethnic, it's in here. Spices and exotic products from around the world are offered at bargain prices. Every foodie worth his (sea) salt knows to come here first.
✚ F7 ✉ 123 Lexington Avenue (28th Street) ☎ 212/685–3451 🚇 6 28th Street

## KAM MAN
The most comprehensive Asian market, with fresh and barbecued meats, dried seafood, jarred sauces, teas, herbs and other exotica.
✚ G14 ✉ 200 Canal Street (Mulberry Street) ☎ 212/571–0330

## ZABAR'S
This is the pleasingly wise-cracking New Yawker of the foodie havens; bigger and more bustling than Dean & DeLuca, with a Jewish soul all its own. Cheese, coffee, smoked fish, breads and the like are downstairs, while upstairs are the city's best buys in kitchenwares.
✚ a6 ✉ 2245 Broadway (80th Street) ☎ 212/787–2000 🚇 1, 9 79th Street

### PICNIC SPOTS
These don't start and end in Central Park. Some more to try, indoors and out:
**Lower Manhattan** Battery Park City—benches and views all along the Hudson South Street Seaport boardwalk.
**SoHo** The "Vest Pocket Park" at Spring and Mulberry streets.
**Greenwich Village** The ballpark at Clarkson and Hudson streets and St. Luke's Garden at Hudson (Barrow/Grove streets) are a well-kept secret—they're perfect!
**Midtown East** Greenacre Park at 51st Street and Second Avenue (what a misnomer). Crystal Pavilion at Third Avenue and 50th Street—atrium with waterfall. Paley Park (53rd Street/Fifth Avenue)—concrete canyon and waterfall.
**Midtown West** Equitable Tower Atrium on Seventh Avenue (51st–52nd streets)—lots of greenery.
**Upper East Side** Carl Shurz Park at East End Avenue (84th–89th streets)—Gracie Mansion, where the mayor lives, is here; also great Roosevelt Island and bridge views.

# Nowhere but New York City

## BOOK WORMS

Although the Barnes & Noble and Border's superstores claim to cover all bases, specialty bookstores abound.
**Biography Book Shop** If your interest lies in people's lives ✉ 400 Bleecker Street ☎ 212/807–8655
**Murder Ink** For mysteries and crime ✉ 2486 Broadway ☎ 212/362–8905
**A Photographer's Place** If you prefer looking at pictures ✉ 133 Mercer Street ☎ 212/431–9358
**Hacker Art Books** If fine art is your thing you can't beat this collection ✉ 45 W57th Street ☎ 212/688–7600
**Books of Wonder** The shelves are filled with children's books ✉ 16 W18th Street ☎ 212/989–3270
**A Different Light Bookstore** Gay and lesbian texts are stocked ✉ 151 W19th Street ☎ 212/989–4850
For other special interests, foreign language books, religious, scholarly or used texts, consult the Manhattan Yellow Pages.

## ABRACADABRA

The largest costume and novelty store anywhere.
✚ E8 ✉ 19 W21st Street (Fifth Avenue) ☎ 212/627–5194 🚇 F Path 23rd Street; N, R 23rd Street

## B&H

Photography superstore with everything you need to take perfect pictures available at good prices.
✚ C5 ✉ 420 Ninth Avenue (34th Street) ☎ 212/444–6625 🚇 A, C, E 34th Street

## ENCHANTED FOREST

Like walking into a fairy tale, this artisanal toy store will enchant adults and kids alike.
✚ F13 ✉ 85 Mercer Street ☎ 212/925–6677 🚇 N, R Prince Street

## FIREFIGHTERS FRIEND

After 11 September this little store was mobbed with fans of America's biggest heroes, snapping up T-shirts, hats, model fire trucks and other NYFD memorabilia.
✚ F12 ✉ 263 Lafayette Street ☎ 212/226–3142 🚇 6 Spring Street

## THE HAT SHOP

Custom-made toppers for women with a distinct downtown flair.
✚ E12 ✉ 120 Thompson Street (Prince Street) ☎ 212/219–1445 🚇 E Spring Street

## J&R

This sprawling complex of stores offers computers, music and office equipment at some of the best prices in town.
✚ F16 ✉ 15–23 Park Row (Beekman Street) ☎ 212/238–9000 🚇 2, 3 Park Place; A, C Broadway–Nassau Street; N, R, 4, 5, 6 City Hall

## JEFFREY NEW YORK

You thought Barney's was the fashion victim's final offer? Jeffrey out-dresses it by a mile. More outré in location (trendy meatmarket), layout (enough space to run a half-marathon) and shoes (many unwearable pairs above $500), it's a must-see if only to gauge what you would be wearing if you cared.
✚ B9 ✉ 449 W14th Street (Tenth Avenue) ☎ 212/206–3928 🚇 A, C 14th Street

## KATE'S PAPERIE

The beautiful handmade stationery paraphernalia is overwhelming at this SoHo boutique.
✚ F12 ✉ 561 Broadway ☎ 212/941–9816 🚇 N, R Prince Street

## KIEHL'S

It's no longer family-owned, but Kiehl's pure personal hygiene products are still great. They give out samples of everything —except the owner's collection of Harley Davidson motorcycles on display.
✚ G9 ✉ 109 Third Avenue (13th Street) ☎ 212/677–3171 🚇 L Third Avenue

## KITCHEN ARTS & LETTERS

Books for the cook and food scholar. Imports and hard-to-find cookbooks are a specialty.
✚ e4 ✉ 1435 Lexington Avenue (94th Street) ☎ 212/876–5550 🚇 4, 5, 6 96th Street

## MAC
If deep, rich, matte make-up colors are what you are looking for, you'll find them at this ultra-trendy boutique.
➕ D10 ✉ 14 Christopher Street ☎ 212/243–4150 🚇 A, B, C, D, E, F W4th Street

## MACKENZIE-CHILDS
Picture Alice in Wonderland meets Rosenthal. Day-glo 3-D ceramics and gifts in an enchanting boutique. The expensive afternoon tea is worth it for the delicious pastries.
➕ d8 ✉ 824 Madison Avenue (69th Street) ☎ 212/570–6050 🚇 6 68th Street

## MAXILLA & MANDIBLE
'Dem bones, 'dem bones. Plus butterflies, antlers and shells.
➕ b6 ✉ 453 Columbus Avenue (81st Street) ☎ 212/724–6173 🚇 C 81st Street

## MICHAEL C. FINA
Every bride wants her list at this exclusive purveyor of gifts, tableware and jewelry.
➕ E4 ✉ 545 Fifth Avenue ☎ 212/557–2500 🚇 4, 5, 6, 7 Grand Central

## MOMA DESIGN STORE
Clever design and clean lines are the emphasis at this gift outlet of the Museum of Modern Art.
➕ E2 ✉ 44 W53rd Street (Fifth Avenue) ☎ 212/767–1050 🚇 E, F Fifth Avenue

## MXYPLYZYK
Modern urban gifts with sleek design and a sense of humor. Beautiful wrapping.
➕ C9 ✉ 125 Greenwich Avenue (12th Street) ☎ 212/989–4300 🚇 A, C, E 14th Street

## PEARL PAINT
Great selection, great prices on art supplies and all related merchandize.
➕ F14 ✉ 308 Canal Street (Broadway) ☎ 212/431–7932 🚇 N, R Canal Street

## POP SHOP
Keith Haring's art for the masses—on umbrellas, tote bags, you name it.
➕ F12 ✉ 292 Lafayette Street (Houston Street) ☎ 212/219–2784 🚇 6 Spring Street

## RICHART
Retail outlet for one of France's most creative chocolatiers—beautiful designs and exotic fillings.
➕ E2 ✉ 7 E55th Street (Fifth Avenue) ☎ 212/371–9369 🚇 E, F Fifth Avenue

## STEUBEN
Retail showroom displaying the work of America's renowned glass artists.
➕ E2 ✉ 717 Fifth Avenue (56th Street) ☎ 212/752–1441 🚇 E, F Fifth Avenue

## TOURNEAU
You may get so caught up in the commotion at this timepiece superstore that you are tempted into over-spending, especially on the layaway (credit) plan.
➕ F1 ✉ 590 Madison Avenue (57th Street) ☎ 212/758–7300 🚇 E, F Fifth Avenue

## ZITOMER
So much more than a pharmacy… there's even a pet department at this posh 50 plus-year-old store.
➕ d8 ✉ 969 Madison Avenue ☎ 212/737–5560 🚇 6 68th Street

## BAGEL PEOPLE
In many cities across the country you can find bagels in such bastardized flavors as blueberry, chocolate or apple crumb. Not so in any self-respecting bagel store in New York. Bagels are a serious matter and they are debated fiercely—there are Ess-A people and there are H&H people. While these are the two reigning kings, there are a couple of others that are worth their salt, or poppy seeds, as the case may be.

### Ess-A-Bagel
✉ 831 Third Avenue ☎ 212/980–1010;
✉ 359 First Avenue ☎ 212/260–2252

### H&H
✉ 2239 Broadway ☎ 212/595–8003;
✉ 639 W46th Street ☎ 212/595–8000

### Columbia Bagels
✉ 2836 Broadway ☎ 212/222–3200

### Pick A Bagel
✉ 1101 Lexington Avenue ☎ 212/517–6500;
✉ 200 W57th Street ☎ 212/957–5151

# Drinks

## DRINK UP

Cocktail culture is alive and well in the Big Apple. The martini craze is here to stay—many bars and lounges offer long menus of creative concoctions with witty names. Elegant glassware is crucial. Atmospheres range from urban chic to clubby lounge to Old New York. Neighborhood pubs, with more emphasis on beer and bourbon, are favorite watering holes. But if you'd rather stay off the hard stuff altogether, you can sit back and relax at any one of the zillion coffee bars around town. But remember, since March 2003, you can't smoke at any of them, licenced or not.

## URBAN CHIC

### FOUR SEASONS HOTEL
I.M. Pei's design gives this a sleek, austere energy. Impressive martini menu and great snacks.
➕ F1 ✉ 57 E57th Street (Lexington Avenue)
☎ 212/758–5700 🚇 4, 5, 6 59th Street

### LOT 61
Giant space with rubber couches and contemporary art on the walls.
➕ B8 ✉ 550 W21st Street (11th Avenue)
☎ 212/243–6555
🚇 C, E 23rd Street

### MERCER HOTEL LOBBY BAR
The friendly modelesque service at this tiny SoHo hotspot makes having a drink a pleasant, chic experience.
➕ F12 ✉ 147 Mercer Street (Prince Street)
☎ 212/966–6060
🚇 N Prince Street

## CLUBBY LOUNGES

### DOUBLE HAPPINESS
The first lounge bar to penetrate Chinatown, this trendy subterranean cocktail den pays homage with Asian tchotchkes (count the abacuses…) and green-tea martinis. Not for quiet conversation.
➕ G13 ✉ 173 Mott Street
☎ 212/941–1282 🚇 6, N, R, Canal Street

### 10TH STREET LOUNGE
Ultra-cool atmosphere with flickering cathedral candles and low couches.
➕ G10 ✉ 212 E10th Street (Second Avenue) ☎ 212/473–5252 🚇 6 Astor Place

## NEIGHBOORHOODY PUBS

### OLD TOWN BAR
Old beer signs, wooden booths and pressed-tin ceilings take you back a century. There's also draft Guinness and tavern food.
➕ F8 ✉ 45 E18th Street (Fifth Avenue/Broadway)
☎ 212/529–6732 🚇 N, R, L, 4, 5, 6 Union Square-14th Street

### WHITE HORSE TAVERN
Dylan Thomas drank his last in this picturesque village pub.
➕ C10 ✉ 567 Hudson Street
☎ 212/243–9260 🚇 1, 9 Christopher Street

### PETE'S TAVERN
This 1864 Gramercy Park Victorian saloon is where O. Henry wrote *The Gift of the Magi*.
➕ F8 ✉ 129 E18th Street
☎ 212/473–7676 🚇 N, R, 4, 6 Union Street

## COFFEE

### DRIP
Drip invented a brand-new singles scene. Browse through the many forms filled out by hopeful dates and, should one catch your fancy, a *barrista* (coffee server) will call them up for you—along with your cup of java.
➕ a5 ✉ 489 Amsterdam Avenue ☎ 212/875–1032
🚇 1, 9 86th Street

### EUREKA JOE'S
A pleasant pitstop with a groaning counter of brownies, wraps, angel cake and so on.
➕ E8 ✉ 168 Fifth Avenue (21st Street) ☎ 212/741–7500 🚇 N, R 23rd Street

# Performance

## BAM

The Brooklyn Academy of Music mounts major cutting-edge extravaganzas in every performing art. There's also a four-screen movie theater and the great BAM Café, with live music.

🚇 Off map ✉ 30 Lafayette Avenue, Brooklyn
☎ 718/636–4100 🚉 A, C Lafayette Avenue

## JOSEPH PAPP PUBLIC THEATER

With two stages, there is always something worth seeing. Recent successes include *Bring in da Noise, Bring in da Funk*.

🚇 F10 ✉ 425 Lafayette Street
☎ 212/598–7150 🚉 F, S Broadway/Lafayette

## THE KITCHEN

An intimate theater for avant-garde performances, from acrobatics to tragic monologues.

🚇 B8 ✉ 512 W19th Street (Eleventh Avenue) ☎ 212/255–5793

## 92ND ST. Y

Cabaret, music, dance and readings are among the happenings here.

🚇 e4 ✉ 1396 Lexington Avenue (92nd Street) ☎ 212/996–1100 🚉 6 96th Street

## PS 122

A converted public school that hosts a wide range of acts from the bizarre to the poignant.

🚇 H10 ✉ First Avenue (9th Street) ☎ 212/477–5288 🚉 N, R 8th Street, F Second Avenue

## SYMPHONY SPACE

Story telling, readings, children's performance, music, dance and more.

🚇 a4 ✉ 2537 Broadway (95th Street) ☎ 212/864–5400 🚉 1, 2, 3, 9 96th Street

## AMATO OPERA

This hollowed-out East Village brownstone mounts full-length grand opera in miniature.

🚇 G11 ✉ 319 Bowery ☎ 212/228–8200 🚉 F Second Avenue

## CARNEGIE HALL

Considered one of the greatest recital halls in the world, Carnegie Hall features an eclectic program ranging from classical artists to folk singers.

🚇 D1 ✉ 881 Seventh Avenue (57th Street) ☎ 212/247–7800 🚉 N, R 57th Street; E Seventh Avenue

## THE METROPOLITAN OPERA

The gala openings at this world-class opera rank among the most glamorous of the city's cultural events. Serious buffs line up on Saturday mornings for inexpensive standing-room tickets. The season runs from October through April.

🚇 a9 ✉ Lincoln Center ☎ 212/362–6000 🚉 1, 9 66th Street

## NEW YORK CITY OPERA

The Met's next-door neighbor, the repertoire of this fine opera company incorporates a wider variety including newer works, operetta and musicals.

🚇 b9 ✉ Lincoln Center ☎ 212/870–5570 🚉 1, 9 66th Street

## SEEING IS BELIEVING

On any given night of the week there is more to do and see in New York than perhaps in any other city in the world. And since movies can cost upward of $10 anyway, you may as well see something live. From the elegance of a grand opera to the excitement of avant-garde performance art, New York spectacles are world-class (even the flops). Broadway shows an expensive, but nothing transports like a great multimillion-dollar musical or an intense performance by a drama diva. Many theaters offer discounts if you buy your tickets at the box office the day of the show or at the TKTS discount ticket outlet (✉ Times Square/47th Street). Be sure to reserve tickets in advance for the most popular shows.

81

# On the Town

## KEEPING UP

One of New York's favorite pastimes is keeping up with what's going on–even if you don't get to see something, you're expected to have an opinion. To stay abreast of what's happening around town, look for extensive weekly listings in *Time Out New York*, *New York* and the *New Yorker* magazines, or the Friday and Sunday editions of *The New York Times* (available on newsstands). You can also pick up free copies of the *Village Voice* and *New York Press* newspapers in storefronts and vestibules around town. The monthly listings in *Paper* magazine have a decidedly downtown focus.

## CABARET

### CAFÉ CARLYLE

This Upper East Side lounge in the elegant Carlyle Hotel is home to Bobby Short, Eartha Kitt and other jazz greats. Bemeleman's Bar next door is less expensive and requires less advance booking.

✚ d7 ✉ Carlyle Hotel, Madison Avenue (76th Street) ☎ 212/570–7189 🚇 6 68th Street

### DON'T TELL MAMA

New names and established performers ranging from comedy to torch singers.

✚ C3 ✉ 343 W46th Street (Ninth Avenue) ☎ 212/757–0788 🚇 A, C, E 42nd Street

### DUPLEX

Drag queens and downtown crooners sit around the piano bar and have a great time.

✚ D10 ✉ 61 Christopher Street (Seventh Avenue) ☎ 212/255–5438 🚇 1, 9 Christopher Street

## COMEDY

### CAROLINE'S ON BROADWAY

Established names will make you either laugh or groan.

✚ D3 ✉ 1626 Broadway (49th Street) ☎ 212/757–4100 🚇 1, 9 50th Street

### GOTHAM COMEDY CLUB

Agreeable venue for up-and-coming comedians.

✚ E8 ✉ 34 W22nd Street (Fifth Avenue) ☎ 212/367–9000 🚇 N, R 23rd Street; F, Path 23rd Street

## JAZZ

### BIRDLAND

Big names, big bands, Coltrane tributes and Cubans is the range here.

✚ C4 ✉ 315 W44th Street ☎ 212/581–3080 🚇 A, C, E 42nd Street Port Authority

### BLUE NOTE

Many big names come to play at this famous club. The cover is high, but the quality of the acts merits it.

✚ E11 ✉ 131 W3rd Street ☎ 212/475–8592 🚇 A, B, C, D, E, F W4th Street

### TONIC

Lower East Side hipsters cram into this atmospheric dive for a mixed bag—from techno via songsters to straight-up jazz.

✚ H12 ✉ 107 Norfolk Street (Delancey/Rivington streets) ☎ 212/358–7503 🚇 F Delancey Street

### VILLAGE VANGUARD

This basement venue is the *ne plus ultra* of divey jazz clubs. The scene is still as hot as the day it opened in 1935.

✚ D8 ✉ 178 Seventh Avenue (11th Street) ☎ 212/255–4037 🚇 1, 9 Christopher Street

## CLUBBING

### APT

Part club, part music venue, part apartment, this hidden (no sign) swanky lounge hosts some wild nights.

✚ B9 ✉ 419 W13th Street (9th and 10th avenues) ☎ 212/414–4245 🚇 A, C 14th Street

### NELL'S

Nell Campbell's two-level

lounge endures, attracting all ages and types.
➕ D9 ✉ 246 W14th Street ☎ 212/675–1567 🚇 A, C, E 14th Street

## S.O.B.'S

The Latin beat keeps you dancing at this tropically decorated nightclub ("Sounds of Brazil"). Also African, reggae and other island music.
➕ D12 ✉ 204 Varick Street ☎ 212/243–4940 🚇 1, 9 Canal Street

## WEBSTER HALL

Huge and still going strong, this is the East Village youth institution.
➕ F10 ✉ 125 E11th Street ☎ 212/353–1600 🚇 N, Q, R, W, 4, 5, 6 Union Square

# MUSIC LOUNGES

## FEZ

Hidden behind the Time Café, upstairs is a *Casablanca*-style Moroccan lounge, downstairs is a contrastingly normal room with booths, tables and a small stage. Thursday's Mingus Big Band (9.30 and 11.30) is the highlight.
➕ F11 ✉ 380 Lafayette Street (E4th Street) ☎ 212/ 533–3000 🚇 F, S Broadway Lafayette; 6 Astor Place

## THE KNITTING FACTORY

The Main Space, the KnitActive Sound Stage, the Old Office and the Tap Bar are the four performance rooms at the leading venue for new music (of all sorts). The basement is the lounge part of the equation.
➕ F14 ✉ 74 Leonard Street (Church Street/Broadway)

☎ 212/219–3055 🚇 1, 9 Franklin Street

# MUSIC VENUES

## BEACON THEATER

Big names fill the marquee at this uptown venue—everything from disco diva Chaka Khan to retro modern rockers the Black Crowes.
➕ a7 ✉ 2124 Broadway (74th Street) ☎ 212/496–7070 🚇 1, 2, 3, 9 72nd Street

## BOWERY BALLROOM

This venue lets the alternative musicians spread out a bit. It is indeed like a ballroom, with a proscenium arch stage.
➕ G13 ✉ 6 Delancey Street (Bowery) ☎ 212/533–2111 🚇 J, M Bowery; 6 Spring Street

## CBGB & OMFUG

This no-frills club gave birth to punk rock and new wave, and it's still going strong.
➕ G11 ✉ 315 Bowery ☎ 212/982–4052 🚇 F Second Avenue

## IRVING PLAZA

You never know who might show up on the calendar for this medium-sized, neighborhoody venue.
➕ F9 ✉ 17 Irving Place ☎ 212/777–6800 🚇 N, R, 4, 6 Union Square

## MERCURY LOUNGE

A laid-back atmosphere that suits eclectic performers. "Lounge" is a misnomer—there are very few seats.
➕ H12 ✉ 217 East Houston Street ☎ 212/260–4700 🚇 F Second Avenue

## NIGHT CRAWLERS

Clubbing in New York is an art form. Most dance clubs don't get going until well after midnight, and some don't stop until noon the next day. Party promoters host different theme nights on different days of the week—each brings a unique crowd: young, old, gay, Latino… Check weekly listings to see what's going on where. Cover charges are steep (upward of $20 at the more popular places) and bouncers are notorious for how harshly they scrutinize the hordes waiting to get in. Being on "the list" means you enter quickly and for free. Don't be intimidated, eventually the doors part for everyone. As a rule, Friday and Saturday nights you'll see mostly suburbanites and tourists; the die-hard New York clubbers prefer Sunday through Wednesday, when the ability to stay out all night is as much about status as it is about having fun. If the sight of people doing drugs, men wearing dresses or people wearing next to nothing at all bothers you, you should probably stay at home.

# Free Summer Entertainment

## SUMMER IN THE CITY

Although New York can be brutally hot in the summer, and the humidity makes it sticky, it does have its upside. Many New Yorkers flee the city each weekend: to shares in the Hamptons, Fire Island or Duchess County. This leaves the city's museums, theaters, nightclubs, bars and restaurants relatively empty for intrepid out-of-towners to explore. But one of the best reasons to brave the summer heat is for the wonderful selection of free entertainment put on by many of the city's premier cultural institutions. Without paying a dime it's possible to enjoy al fresco operas, theater, art, eating, jazz, classical music, movies, dance, rock-and-roll, blues and folk music. Many arrive early for big performances and stake out a spot for a picnic. For events on the Great Lawn, in Central Park, the sky over the area is filled with colored balloons that clever picnickers fly from their spots to indicate to their friends where they are.

## MUSIC

### CENTRAL PARK SUMMER STAGE

Fantastic free concerts. The line-up has included Tracy Chapman, David Byrne and countless other music-world luminaries.
➕ d8  ✉ Naumberg Bandshell (72nd Street)  ☎ 212/360–2777  🕐 Jun–Aug  🚇 C 72nd Street

### LINCOLN CENTER OUT-OF-DOORS (➤ 41)

Summer-long program that includes music, dance, educational activities and art.
☎ 212/875–5400

### METROPOLITAN OPERA IN THE PARK

A whole season of free park concerts on the great lawn—truly a gala affair.
☎ 212/870–7492

### NEW YORK PHILHARMONIC

As above.
☎ 212/721–6500  🕐 Jul–Aug

### PROSPECT PARK BANDSHELL (➤ 30)

Enter at Prospect Park West and 9th Street to find Brooklyn's summer stage.
☎ 718/965–8999

## THEATER

### SHAKESPEARE IN THE PARK

You have to wait in line for tickets to these free world-class outdoor productions. Why not make a day of it and bring a picnic lunch?
➕ c6  ✉ Delacorte Theater, Central Park  ☎ 212/875–5709  🕐 Jul–Aug  🚇 B, C 81st Street

### HBO SUMMER FESTIVAL AT BRYANT PARK

Monday nights throughout summer movies are shown on a giant screen.
➕ E4  ☎ 212/983–4142

## DANCING

### MIDSUMMER NIGHT SWING

"Dances under the Stars" is the subtitle for this weekly public party.
➕ a9  ✉ Lincoln Center Plaza  ☎ 212/875–5400  🕐 Jun–Jul  🚇 1, 9 66th Street

## FESTIVALS

### FOURTH OF JULY

Celebrations kick off at the Stars and Stripes Regatta
✉ South Street Seaport  ☎ 212/669–9400  🕐 3–4 Jul
At night the New York Philharmonic plays in Central Park, with a firework finale ☎ 212/875–5030, and Macy's shoots millions of dollars into the sky over the Lower Hudson ☎ 212/494–5432. Good vantage points get very crammed; consider Brooklyn.

### MUSEUM MILE FESTIVAL

Perambulate Fifth Avenue visiting museums for free. The street is blocked off, giving a party feel.
➕ d5  🕐 6–9pm throughout Jun  🚇 4, 5, 6 86th Street

### NINTH AVENUE INTERNATIONAL FOOD FESTIVAL

Ethnic eateries sell samples from street stands.
➕ C3  ☎ 800/894–9166  🕐 10am–7pm, 3rd weekend in May  🚇 C, E 50th Street

# Take Me Out to the Ball Game

### THE GIANTS AND THE JETS

New York's beloved football teams, who both play at the same stadium. The Giants last won the Superbowl in 1991, but the Jets haven't been champions since 1969. It's difficult to get tickets, as most are used by season ticket-holders.

✉ Giants Stadium, Meadowlands
☎ 201/935–3900

### METROSTARS

Though soccer is not a popular sport in the US, the MetroStars are slowly building a following. Many fans are transplanted Europeans or South Americans.

✉ Giants Stadium, Meadowlands
☎ 201/460–4355

### THE KNICKS

New Yorkers are fiercely loyal to this hometown basketball team. Lots of fans bring binoculars to the games, partly to watch celebs like Spike Lee and Woody Allen, who have courtside seats.

✉ Madison Square Garden
☎ Knicks Hotline 212/465–JUMP

### THE RANGERS

The city's favorite hockey team (except for Islander fans). In 1994 they won the coveted Stanley Cup.

✉ Madison Square Garden
☎ Rangers Hotline 212/308–NYRS

### THE ISLANDERS

In the 1980s the Islanders hockey team reigned, much to the joy of their (mostly Long Island) fans.

✉ Nassau Coliseum
☎ 516/888–9000

### THE YANKEES

Despite talk of moving the team to Manhattan they still play in "the house that Ruth built" in the Bronx, and Yankee Stadium (▶ 49) is still awe inspiring. The Yankees have won more World Series championships than any other baseball team, and have truly defined what it is to be a sports dynasty.

✉ Yankee Stadium
☎ 718/293–6000
🚇 #4 161st Street

### THE METS

There are Yankee fans and there are Mets fans. The Mets started playing in 1962 and won the hearts of New Yorkers with their World Series victory in 1969. Since then the city has been largely divided in their loyalties.

✉ Shea Stadium
☎ 718/507–8499

### THE NEW JERSEY NETS AND THE NEW JERSEY DEVILS

Though these teams (basketball and hockey respectively) are not from New York, they play only minutes away. The closeness of the teams to New York creates a "cross-town rivalry" that is always fun for fans to follow.

✉ Continental Airlines Arena at Meadowlands
☎ 201/935–3900

### USTA NATIONAL TENNIS CENTER

This public tennis facility is home to the US Open, where the world's tennis greats compete in August.

☎ 718/760–6200
🚇 #7 Willets Point/Shea Stadium

### OUTDOOR ACTIVITY IN CENTRAL PARK

Despite Manhattan's reputation as an asphalt jungle, Central Park is one of the most welcoming parks in the world. For those who crave physical activity there's plenty to do.

**Bike Riding** You can rent no-frills bicycles and join the hordes cycling around the Park's 6-mile (10km) loop.

**Roller Blading** Skate rental and lessons are available at Wollman Rink, or you can try your luck on your own. Watch out for the hills.

**Ice Skating** Wollman Rink rents figure skates and hockey skates and is an ice rink in winter. There's a snack bar where you can retreat when it gets too cold (☎ 212/396–1010).

**Running** The most popular place for running and jogging. On New Year's Eve there is an organized Midnight Run that is part costume ball, part fireworks display and part 5-mile (8km) race. Runners are toasted with champagne—a great way to ring in the new year.

# Luxury Hotels

## PRICES

Expect to pay the following prices per night for a double room:

Luxury      over $325
Mid-range   $160–$325
Budget      under $160

## THE NEW STYLE OF LUXURY

Traditionally New York's priciest hotels have offered traditional amenities in conservative, formal settings. In the last two decades however, a crop of ultra-chic hotels opened around the city that offer guests truly luxurious amenities in modern, stylish settings. The first was the Royalton, which started the trend in 1987. A steady trickle followed…then the deluge. In 2000 alone 10 modern grand hotels opened in Manhattan. The hotels not only offer hip accommo-dations and grand services, but also restaurants, lounges and bars that attract trendy New Yorkers from all corners of the city.

## BRYANT PARK

The landmark American Radiator Building in Bryant Park was redesigned by hip minimalist architect David Chipperfield and opened in 2001 as a super-swanky 129-room hotel. It has a gym, private screening theater and famous chef Rick Laakonen.
➕ E4  ✉ 40 W40th Street
☎ 212/869–0100;
fax: 212/869–4446;
www.bryantparkhotel.com
🍴 Ilo  🚇 B, D, F, Q 42nd Street

## CHAMBERS

This 77-room hotel (opened spring 2001) has a downtown soul but a Midtown address. Contemporary art is everywhere and the decor is industrial chic. The restaurant, designed by David Rockwell, boasts chef Geoffrey Zakarian.
➕ E2  ✉ 15 W55th Street
☎ 212/974–5656;
fax: 212/974–5657;
www.chambershotel.com
🍴 Town  🚇 B, Q 57th Street

## FOUR SEASONS

Part of the chain, this I.M. Pei designed masterpiece redefines grandeur. The soaring entrance may in-duce vertigo, but the 370 lovely rooms and suites, with marble bathrooms, will offer calm relief.
➕ F1  ✉ 57 E57th Street, Midtown East ☎ 212/758–5700; fax: 212/758–5711; www.fourseasons.com 🍴 5757
🚇 B, Q 57th Street

## THE MARK

This exquisite and peace-ful townhouse-mansion, a couple of blocks from the park on the Upper East Side, has antiques, goose-down pillows, palms and Piranesi prints in most of the 180 rooms and suites.
➕ d7  ✉ 25 E77th Street
☎ 212/744–4300; fax: 212/744–2749; www.themarkhotel.com 🍴 Mark's 🚇 6 77th Street

## MERCER HOTEL

A favorite among young celebrities, the 75-room Mercer exudes glamour. Some deluxe rooms have a deep, freestanding marble tub in the bathroom.
➕ F12  ✉ 147 Mercer Street (Prince Street) ☎ 212/966–6060; fax: 212/965–3838; www.mercerhotel.com 🍴 Mercer Kitchen 🚇 N, R Prince Street

## THE PLAZA

A byword for grand hotel, renovations have kept The Plaza up to date in comfort. The hotel is child-friendly, with kids' programs laid on. Park view rooms are best. 692 rooms, 112 suites.
➕ E1  ✉ Fifth Avenue (Central Park South) ☎ 212/759–3000; fax: 212/546–5324; www.plazahotel.com 🍴 Oak Room 🚇 N, R 5th Avenue

## ST. REGIS

Formal Louis XV style makes this a bona-fide oasis in the middle of Midtown. The service is discreet and thorough, and the 221 rooms and 92 suites are plush. In the famous King Cole Bar gentlemen puff cigars under a Maxfield Parrish mural. Fitness club.
➕ E2  ✉ 2 E55th Street (Fifth/Madison avenues) ☎ 212/753–4500; fax: 212/ 787–3447; www.starwood.com/stregis 🍴 Lespinasse 🚇 6 51st Street

# Mid-Range Hotels

### HOTEL BEACON
Located smack in the middle of Broadway, on the Upper West Side, the Beacon feels more like an apartment building than a hotel. The 200-plus rooms are large and some have kitchenettes.
✚ a7 ✉ 2130 Broadway (75th Street) ☎ 212/787–1100; fax: 212/724–0839; www.beaconhotel.com 🍽 1, 2, 3 72nd Street

### FITZPATRICK
This 92-room hotel on the easterly side of Midtown has Irish charm in abundance. It stands out for service, good taste—and the perfect brunch.
✚ F1 ✉ 687 Lexington Avenue ☎ 212/355–0100; fax: 212/308–5166; www.fitzpatrickhotels.com 🍽 Fitzers 🚇 4, 6 59th Street

### FRANKLIN
In the heart of Upper East Side, this lovely boutique hotel offers a luxurious setting close to the city's major museums, Central Park and shopping on Madison Avenue. The 47 small, comfortable rooms are tastefully furnished.
✚ e5 ✉ 164 E87th Street ☎ 212/369–1000; fax: 212/369–8000; www.franklinhotel.com 🚇 4, 5, 6 86th Street

### THE HUDSON
Ridiculously trendy the moment it opened (in late 2000), Ian Schrager's fourth New York address has 1,000 rooms and all the expected accouterments. There's the Hudson Cafeteria and the Bar, complete with glowing yellow dance floor and outside courtyard, plus a David Barton gym with a pool, bowling alley and archery. On the downside, the mirror-and-mahogany-walled rooms are small.
✚ C1 ✉ 356 W58th Street ☎ 212/554–6000; fax: 212/554–6001; www.hudsonhotel.com 🍽 Hudson Cafeteria 🚇 A, B, C, D, 1, 9 Columbus Circle

### MAYFLOWER
A classic hotel offering comfort and charm in a residential neighborhood near the Lincoln Center. Many of the 365 rooms have spectacular views of Central Park.
✚ b9 ✉ Central Park West (61st Street) ☎ 212/265–0060; fax: 212/265–2026; www.mayflowerhotel.com 🍽 The Conservatory 🚇 A, C, D 1 59th Street

### THE SHOREHAM
The sleek Shoreham hotel has 174 small but cozy rooms, with ultra-suede walls, diffused lighting and puffy white comforters on the beds.
✚ E2 ✉ 33 W55th Street ☎ 212/247–6700; fax: 212/765–9741; www.shorehamhotel.com 🚇 B, Q 57th Street

### W UNION SQUARE
The largest and most luxe of the four NYC "W" hotels, with trays of grass, gray-and-white decor, high-speed data ports and Aveda products in the 270 rooms. The Underbar is a townies' hangout and Boston's Todd English runs the eatery.
✚ F9 ✉ 201 Park Avenue ☎ 212/253–9119; fax: 212/253–9229; www.whotels.com 🍽 Olives 🚇 4, 5, 6, N, R, L Union Square 14th Street

### THE ALGONQUIN
The Algonquin is forever associated with the only group of literary wits to be named after a piece of furniture: the Algonquin Round Table. Not quite the Bloomsbury Group, the *bon viveurs* achieved almost as much at the bar here as they did in the pages of the embryo *New Yorker*, with Robert Benchley, Dorothy Parker and Alexander Woollcott particularly well ensconced. The hotel's Rose Room still contains the very table, though the *New Yorker* offices no longer decant straight into the hotel since they moved into the chilly, modern Condé Nast tower.

# Budget Hotels

## B&BS

Those who prefer real neighborhoods, authentic experiences and behaving like a local may opt for a B&B. Often these are found in Brooklyn brownstones, where the host has an extra room. Others are empty apartments. The only imperative is to reserve ahead.

**Abode Bed and Breakfasts Ltd** ✉ Box 20022, NY 10028 ☎ 212/472–2000
**At Home in New York** ☎ 212/956–3125
**Bed and Breakfast Network of New York** ✉ 134 W32nd Street, Suite 602 ☎ 212/645–8134
**Inn New York** ✉ 266 W71st Street ☎ 212/580–1900
**New World Bed and Breakfast** ✉ 150 Fifth Avenue, Suite 711 ☎ 212/675–5600
**Urban Ventures** ✉ Box 426, NY 10024 ☎ 212/594–5650
**West Village Reservations** ☎ 212/614–3034

## CARLTON ARMS

Decorated with crazy murals by artist guests, this is perhaps the wackiest hotel in New York. Amenities are minimal but there is a communal atmosphere that makes solo travelers feel at home. As it says on the business card "this ain't no Holiday Inn." 54 rooms.
➕ G7 ✉ 160 E25th Street ☎ 212/684–8337; www.carltonarms.com 🚇 6 23rd Street

## CHELSEA SAVOY

Friendly 90-room hotel in the heart of Chelsea offering clean, no-frills accommodations and a continental breakfast.
➕ D8 ✉ 204 W23rd Street ☎ 212/929–9253; fax: 212/741–6309 🚇 1, 9 23rd Street

## GERSHWIN

"We're just at the edge of hip," says the manager of this first New York Interclub hotel—Urs Jakob's string of super-hostels. Art elevates the style of the 150 basic rooms; bars, roofdecks and lounges encourage sociability.
➕ E7 ✉ 7 E27th Street ☎ 212/545–8000; fax: 212/684–5546; www.gershwinhotel.com 🍴 Café 🚇 N, R 23rd Street

## HOTEL BELLECLAIRE

Mark Twain lived here, as well as Maxim Gorky. Now the early 20th-century building offers 167 clean, minimal guest rooms for ordinary travelers, with simple pine furniture and pale apricot-colored walls. It's in a quiet, residential area and the lovely Riverside Park is next door.
➕ a7 ✉ 250 W77th Street ☎ 212/362–7700; fax: 212/362–1004; www.hotelbelleclaire.com 🚇 1, 9 79th Street

## OLCOTT

A much-loved New York address for many performing artists, thanks to its Lincoln Center proximity and very reasonable rates. The Olcott's 150 rooms are mostly suites, complete with kitchenettes and often a separate living room with TV. It's shabby but homey. There's a three-night minimum stay.
➕ b7 ✉ 27 W72nd Street ☎ 212/877–4200; fax: 212/580–0511; www.hotelolcott.com 🚇 1, 2, 3, 9 72nd Street

## SEAPORT INN

Part of the Best Western chain, this 72-room hotel offers predictable comfort. Located near the South Street Seaport, with easy access to lower Manhattan.
➕ G16 ✉ 33 Peck Slip ☎ 212/766–6600; fax: 212/766–6615; www.stay-at-our-charming-new-york-hotel.com 🚇 2, 3, 4 Fulton Street

## WASHINGTON SQUARE

Overlooking Washington Square Park, this is the only hotel in the heart of Greenwich Village. Despite the recent renovation, the amenities are still minimal. 165 rooms.
➕ E10 ✉ 103 Waverley Place ☎ 212/777–9515; fax: 212/979–8373; www.washingtonsquarehotel.com 🍴 CIII 🚇 1, 9 Christopher Street

# NEW YORK CITY
## travel facts

## Essential Facts

### Customs
- Non-US citizens may import duty free: 1 quart (just under a liter) of alcohol (no-one under 21 can import alcohol), 200 cigarettes or 50 cigars and $100 of gifts.
- Have a doctor's certificate for any medication you are taking with you.
- Among restricted items for import are meat, fruit, plants, seeds and lottery tickets.

### Electricity
- The supply is 100 volts, 60 cycles AC current.
- US appliances use two-prong plugs. European appliances require an adapter.

### Etiquette
- Tipping: waitstaff get 15–20 percent (roughly double the 8.25 percent sales tax at the bottom of the bill); so do cab drivers. Bartenders get about the same (though less than $1 is stingy) and will probably "buy" you a drink if you're there a while. Bellhops ($1 per bag), room service waiters (10 percent), and hairdressers (15–20 percent) should also be tipped.
- Panhandlers: you will need a strategy for distributing change to the panhandlers among New York's immense homeless population. Some New Yorkers give once a day; some carry pockets of pennies; some give food; others give to a charity.
- Smoking is no longer a matter of politeness; there are stringent smoking laws in New York. Smoking is banned on all public transportation, in cabs and in all places of work, including restaurants and bars.

### Lavatories
- Don't use public lavatories on the street, in stations or in subways.
- Public buildings provide locked bathrooms (ask the doorman, cashier or receptionist for the key). Otherwise use lavatories in hotel lobbies, bars or restaurants.

### Money matters
- Credit cards are a widely accepted. Visa, MasterCard, American Express, Diner's Card and Discover are the most commonly used cards.
- Traveler's checks are accepted in all but small stores; $20 and $50 denominations are the most useful. Don't bother trying to exchange these at the bank—it is more trouble than it's worth, and commissions are high.

### Opening hours
- Banks: Mon–Fri 9–3 or 3.30; some are open longer, and on Saturday.
- Stores: Mon–Sat 10–6; many are open far later, and on Sunday; those in the Villages, Nolita and SoHo open and close later.
- Museums: hours vary, but Monday is the most common closing day.
- Post offices: Mon–Fri 10–5 or 6.
- Of course, in the city that never sleeps, you'll find much open around the clock.

### Places of worship
- Baptist: Memorial Baptist Church ✉ 141 W115th Street ☎ 212/663–8830; tourists are welcomed (for a moderate charge) Sundays 10.45am.
- Episcopal: Cathedral of St. John the Divine ✉ 112th Street (Amsterdam Avenue) ☎ 212/316–7400; services at 8, 9, 11am, 7pm. Grace Church ✉ 802 Broadway (10th Street) ☎ 212/254–2000; services at 9 and 11am.
- Jewish: Temple Emanu-El

✉ 1 E65th Street ☎ 212/744–1400;
services at 5.30pm.
- Methodist: Christ Church United
  Methodist ✉ Park Avenue (60th Street)
  ☎ 212/838–3036; services 9 and 11am.
- Roman Catholic: St. Patrick's
  Cathedral ✉ Fifth Avenue (50th Street)
  ☎ 212/753–2261

## Students

- An International Student Identity
  Card (ISIC) is good for reduced
  admission at many museums,
  theaters and other attractions.
- Carry the ISIC or some other
  photo ID card at all times, to
  prove you're over 21, or you could
  be denied admission to nightclubs
  or be unable to buy liquor.
- Under-25s will find it hard to rent
  a car.

## PUBLIC TRANSPORTATION

### Buses

- Buses are safe, clean—and
  excruciatingly slow. The fastest
  are Limited Stop buses.
- Ask the driver for a transfer that
  entitles you to a free onward or
  crosstown journey for an hour
  after boarding using the intersec-
  ting services listed on the back.
- A bus map showing many of the
  200 routes traveled by the blue
  and white buses is essential.

### Subway

- Since the recent clean-up, cars are
  free of that famous dangerous-
  looking graffiti and are air-
  conditioned. Still, the system is
  confusing at first, and you will
  probably manage some mistakes.
- Children under 44in (113cm) tall
  ride free.
- Transit information ☎ 718/330–1234
  🕐 6am–9pm; www.mta.info
- Avoid the less populated subway

lines at night. If you do ride at
night, stay in the "off hour waiting
area" until your train arrives.

## Taxis

- Cab drivers are notorious for (a)
  knowing nothing about New York
  geography, (b) not speaking
  English and (c) having an
  improvisational driving style.
- Tip 15 percent. Bills larger than
  $10 are unpopular for short
  journeys.
- For more information on public
  transportation ➤ 7.

## DRIVING

- Driving in New York is not
  recommended, but a car is essential for excursions further afield.
- The address of the nearest major
  car-rental outlet can be found by
  calling the following toll-free
  numbers: Avis ☎ 800/331–1212;
  Budget 800/527–0700;
  Hertz ☎ 800/654–3080;
  Thrifty ☎ 800/367–2277
- If driving in New York is unavoid-
  able, make sure you understand
  the restrictions because penalties
  for infringements are stringent. In
  many streets parking alternates
  daily from one side to the other,
  and it is illegal to park within 10ft
  (3m) either side of a fire hydrant.
  A car illegally parked will be towed
  away and the driver heavily fined.
  Within the city limits right turns at
  a red light are prohibited and the
  speed limit is 30mph (48kph). Pas-
  sing a stopped school bus is illegal
  and stiff fines can be imposed.

## MEDIA & COMMUNICATIONS

### Newspapers & magazines

- The local papers are the *New
  York Times* (with a huge Sunday

91

edition), the *Daily News* (also with a generously supplemented Sunday edition) and the *New York Post*. Also look for the respected *Wall Street Journal* and the pink-hued, gossip-heavy, weekly *New York Observer*.

- As well as the *New Yorker*, *New York* and *Time Out*, you may also see the self-consciously hip *The Paper*, the glossy *Manhattan File* and the even glossier *Avenue*.

## Post offices

- The main post office ✉ **Eighth Avenue (33rd Street)** ☎ **212/967–8585** is open 24 hours. Branch post offices are listed in Yellow Pages ◷ **Mon–Fri 8–6, Sat 8–1**
- Stamps are also available from hotel concierges and vending machines in stores, for a 25 percent surcharge.

## Radio & television

- New York's excellent National Public Radio station, WNYC, broadcasts classical and avant-garde music, as well as jazz, news and cultural programing on FM 93.9, and AM 820.
- The most famous of New York's "shock jocks" is Howard Stern, who broadcasts Mon–Fri 6–10am on FM 92.3 WXRK.
- Hotels usually receive many cable channels, if not the hundreds now available to digital subscribers.
- Other channels include New York 1 (with its constant onscreen weather update) and home shopping, as well as the live drama of Court TV.

## Telephones

- Public pay phones are everywhere, and nearly always work.
- All New York numbers require the prefix to be dialled (212, 718,

646 or 917). As with all long-distance calls, add a "1" before the code.
- Hotels can levy hefty surcharges, even on local calls, so use payphones instead or the long-distance services of AT&T, MCI and Sprint that make calling home relatively convenient and let you avoid the surcharges; typically, you dial an 800 number.
- Prepaid phonecards are widely available in stores, and there are a few credit card phones.
- To call the US from the UK, dial 001. To call the UK from the US, dial 011 44, then drop the first zero from the area code.

## EMERGENCIES

### Emergency phone numbers

- Police, Fire Department, Ambulance ☎ 911
- Police, Fire Department, Ambulance for the deaf ☎ 800/342–4357
- Crime Victims Hotline ☎ 212/577–7777
- Sex Crimes Report Line ☎ 212/267–7273

### Consulates

- Australia ✉ 636 Fifth Avenue ☎ 212/245–4000
- Canada ✉ 1251 Sixth Avenue ☎ 212/586–2400
- Denmark ✉ 825 Third Avenue ☎ 212/223–4545
- France ✉ 934 Fifth Avenue ☎ 212/606–3600
- Germany ✉ 460 Park Avenue ☎ 212/308–8700
- Ireland ✉ 515 Madison Avenue ☎ 212/319–2555
- Italy ✉ 690 Park Avenue ☎ 212/737–9100
- Netherlands ✉ 1 Rockefeller Plaza

☎ 212/249–1429
- Norway ✉ 825 Third Avenue
  ☎ 212/421–7333
- Sweden ✉ Dag Hammarskjøld Plaza
  ☎ 212/751–5900
- UK ✉ 845 Third Avenue ☎ 212/752–8400

## Lost Property
- You are unlikely to recover something you lose, but try the following:
  Subway and bus ☎ 718/625–6200
  Taxi ☎ 212/840–4734
  J.F.K. ☎ 718/656–4120
  Newark ☎ 201/961–2230
  You should report any loss as soon as possible if you plan to claim on your insurance.

## Medical treatment
- It is essential to have adequate insurance coverage (► 7).
- In the event of an emergency, the 911 operator will send an ambulance.
- The Doctors on Call service ☎ 212/737–2333 is 24 hours
- Near Midtown, 24-hour emergency rooms are open at:
  St. Luke's-Roosevelt Hospital
  ✉ 58th Street (Ninth Avenue)
  ☎ 212/523–6800
  St. Vincent's Hospital
  ✉ Seventh Avenue (11th Street)
  ☎ 212/604–7997
- Dental Emergency Service
  ☎ 212/679–3966, after 8pm 212/679–4172

## Medicines
- Bring a prescription or doctor's certificate, as well as your current supply for any medications you already take, in case of loss.
- Drugstores that are open for 24 hours include Duane Reade
  ✉ 485 Lexington Avenue (47th Street)
  ☎ 212/682–5338; ✉ 224 W57th Street (Broadway) ☎ 212/541–9708;
  Kaufman's Pharmacy ✉ Lexington

Avenue (50th Street) ☎ 212/755–2266;
and Genovese ✉ Second Avenue (68th Street) ☎ 212/772–0104

## Sensible precautions
- Maintain an awareness of your surroundings and of other people, and try to look as though you know your way around.
- Don't get involved with street crazies, however entertaining they may be.
- The less populated subway lines are best avoided at night, and also Alphabet City east of Avenue C, the far west of Midtown and north of about 110th Street.
- Central Park is a no-go area after dark (except for performances), and the Financial District is eerily deserted—it's generally best to avoid deserted places at night.
- Apart from this, common-sense rules—conceal your wallet; keep the fastener of your bag on the inside; don't let your handbag dangle over the back of your chair; and don't flash large amounts of cash or jewelry.
- New York women are street-wise and outspoken, so if you are a woman on your own and someone's bugging you, tell him to get lost—he'll be expecting it.

## VISITOR INFORMATION
- NYC & Company (formerly the New York Convention & Visitors' Bureau) provides free bus and subway maps, calendars of events and discount coupons for Broadway shows ✉ 810 Seventh Avenue, 3rd floor ☎ 212/484–1200 ◷ Mon–Fri 9–6, weekends 10–3
- Much information is available on the official New York City website (www.nyc.gov), though most is geared toward residents.

# Index

# CityPack
## New York Top 25

### ABOUT THE AUTHOR

Adopted New Yorker Kate Sekules writes about travel, food and fitness for many magazines, including the *New Yorker*, *Travel & Leisure*, *Health & Fitness*, *Food & Wine* and *Harper's Bazaar*. She is also a co-author of Fodor's *New York City*, author of *By Night: New York* and a consultant on the US Mobil Travel Guides.

| CONTRIBUTIONS TO LIVING NEW YORK | Jessica Blatt |
| OVER DESIGN | Tïgïst Getachew, Fabrizio La Rocca |
| CONTRIBUTIONS TO 'WHERE TO...' | The James Beard Foundation |

A CIP catalogue record for this book is available from the British Library.

**ISBN 0 7495 4016 8**

The contents of this publication are believed correct at the time of printing. Nevertheless, the publishers cannot be held responsible for any errors or omissions or for changes in the details given in this guide or for the consequences of any reliance on the information provided by the same. Assessments of attractions, hotels, restaurants and so forth are based upon the author's own personal experience and, therefore, descriptions given in this guide necessarily contain an element of subjective opinion which may not reflect the publishers' opinion or dictate a reader's own experiences on another occasion. We have tried to ensure accuracy in this guide, but things do change so we would be grateful if readers would advise us of any inaccuracies they may encounter.

Published by AA Publishing (a trading name of Automobile Association Developments Limited, whose registered office is Millstream, Maidenhead Road, Windsor, Berkshire, SL4 5GD. Registered number 1878835).

**© AUTOMOBILE ASSOCIATION DEVELOPMENTS LIMITED 1996, 1997, 1999, 2002, 2004**

First published 1996. Revised second edition 1997. Reprinted Mar, Nov, Dec 1998 and Jan, Mar 1999. Revised third edition 1999. Revised fourth edition 2002. Revised fifth edition 2004. Reprinted 2004.

Colour separation by Daylight Colour Art Pte Ltd, Singapore

Printed and bound by Hang Tai D&P Limited, Hong Kong.

### ACKNOWLEDGEMENTS

The Automobile Association would like to thank the following photographers, libraries and associations for their assistance in the preparation of this book: AKG LONDON 17r; ALLSPORT (UK) Ltd 49t (D Strohmeyer), 49b (O Greule); THE BRIDGEMAN ART LIBRARY, LONDON 16l plan of Manhattan, British Library, London, 171 George Washington by Gilbert Stuart, Metropolitan Museum of Art, New York, 17c The Unveiling of the Statue of Liberty, 1886 by Edward Moran, Museum of the City of New York; THE FRICK COLLECTION 43b; ROBERT HARDING PICTURE LIBRARY 18/9; KATHY LOCKLEY 16r; NEW YORK CONVENTION AND VISITORS' BUREAU, INC. 62; PICTOR INTERNATIONAL, LONDON 8bl; ELLEN ROONEY 61; STOCKBYTE 5. The remaining photographs are held in the Association's own library (AA PHOTO LIBRARY) and were taken by SIMON MCBRIDE with the exception of the following: DOUGLAS CORRANCE cover: Circle Line boat, Statue of Liberty, Flatiron Building, yellow cab, skyscraper 1t, 2, 4, 6ll, 29b, 31b, 32, 35b, 37r, 42, 46t, 46b, 51t, 53, 55; RICHARD G ELLIOT cover: Chrysler Building, St Patrick's cathedral, 22rc, 26r, 28, 29t, 31t, 34, 36, 37b, 39r, 40, 43t, 44, 45t, 45b, 47, 48, 54, 57, 63b, 89t; PAUL KENWARD cover: Rockefeller Center, 20/1, 22r, 25, 26b, 27, 30, 33t, 33b, 35t, 38, 39b, 41, 50, 51l, 51b, 52, 59, 60, 63t, 89b; ELLEN ROONEY 23bl; CLIVE SAWYER 9r, 10t, 12t, 14t, 16t, 18tl, 20tl, 22tl, 23t.

A02166

Maps © Automobile Association Developments Limited 1996, 2004
Fold out map © Automobile Association Developments Limited 2002
Transport map © TCS, Aldershot, England

### TITLES IN THE CITYPACK SERIES

- Amsterdam • Bangkok • Barcelona • Beijing • Berlin • Boston • Brussels & Bruges •
- Chicago • Dublin • Florence • Hong Kong • Lisbon • Ljubljana • London • Los Angeles •
- Madrid • Melbourne • Miami • Montréal • Munich • New York • Paris • Prague • Rome •
- San Francisco • Seattle • Shanghai • Singapore • Sydney • Tokyo • Toronto • Venice •
- Vienna • Washington DC •